So – WHY Do You Homeschool?

Answering Questions People Ask About Home Education

By

Mimi Davis

Dedication

This book is lovingly dedicated to Linda B. Murphy, PhD., who taught me the importance of thinking outside the box, and what it is to be a true pioneer in education. Thanks, Mom.

A special thank you goes out to my family for the patience they have shown me in this process. I couldn't have done this without you. You are all such an incredible blessing.

I would also like to extend a thank you to each member of my "editing party." You know who you are. I appreciate the hard work and dedication you showed.

Table of Contents

Preface

There are a lot of books about homeschooling on the shelves of bookstores. Why should I write <u>this</u> book? Well, most of those books were written for home educators. This one, however, was written to be readable by those who don't teach their children at home, although I hope it's useful for home educators, too.

If you are a close relative, distant relative, neighbor, friend or acquaintance of a homeschooler, and you want to know why anyone would want to educate their children at home, or who have other questions you want (or *don't* want...!) to ask your homeschooling friends, this book is for you. It's also for your homeschooling friends. Most homeschoolers spend a lot of time answering questions from concerned friends and family members, as well as from strangers. Hopefully, this will give them some insight into how to respond to strangers, and maybe even help them find answers to some of the harder questions for the first time. It also reviews some recent research that's not available in older books.

I know it's hard to slog through a lot of technical language, so I've tried to make this friendly and readable. On the other hand, it takes research to answer some questions. I've tried to make this usable for those who just want to look at a few questions as a reference, as well as those who expect to read it from cover to cover. That's why the sections are organized into questions under general topics. That does means there may be some repetition of information. I hope I have found a good balance.

One disclaimer: I have tried to represent homeschoolers from a variety of perspectives, but of course, I can only answer questions in depth from my own perspective. There is no way I can address ALL the questions people have about the complicated process of homeschooling in one book, and the answers I give may not completely apply to you, your friends or family. *My* opinions, of course, will be heavily represented, and may not represent the opinions of other homeschoolers you know. However, there's also a lot of good information here, and I hope it will give you some assurance that home educators haven't completely fallen off the deep end.

In addition, I'm writing this book to explain the good points about home education to those who may not be aware of them. Therefore, I often contrast ideal homeschooling with less-than-ideal traditional schooling. That's not because I am anti-school or because I think everyone should homeschool; I don't. I am simply making the point that homeschooling can compare very favorably with traditional schools, and that there are many reasons why people would choose to homeschool. Many families are very happy with their school situations and should keep doing what they're doing. I'm not trying to change that. I'm describing circumstances that have pushed others, who are *not* happy with *their* school situations, to make the homeschooling choice.

Another point: Homeschoolers use a lot of different words to describe what they do. Although there is some controversy about the differences between home education, homeschooling, home teaching, etc., I have used these phrases interchangeably in this book. I'm just talking about education that occurs out of the context of schools and is directed and monitored by parents or guardians. I will probably show a little bit of a preference for the phrase home education, since much learning occurs without school-like influence. In home education circles, the term is often written 'homeschooling,' so I have used it, too, even though my computer's spell-check objects.

My Story

$\looparrowright$

I currently teach my children at home, but I have not always been a home educator. I am a certified special education teacher, and have taught in many settings, including a psychiatric hospital, a resource room in a public school, a private school for children with "learning differences", and a chemical dependency (i.e., drug rehabilitation) program for court-involved children from as young as 5th grade through seniors in high school. I have worked and volunteered in a wide variety of educational situations, taking positions such as a camp counselor for handicapped citizens, a house parent at a group home for autistic adults, an aide in a middle school for special needs children and an aide in a preschool program for language delayed preschoolers. My major in college was in severe and profound handicapping conditions, so I had experiences with very handicapped children as well.

My mom is a professional educator, too. In fact, she's a teacher educator (which just means she's involved in the process of teaching teachers how to teach and certifying them). She has served as the Dean of the College of Education at three universities, taught biology and English, and has worked as a school psychologist. In other words, I have a strong background in the field of professional education.

I became aware of home education about fifteen years ago. I really became interested in it when I had the opportunity to test some home educated children for a local homeschool program. The children I met performed better on tests than those I had tested in schools, and those who had always been home educated tested better than those who were just being removed from the school system. Even "special needs" children were doing better than I expected. This perked my interest.

Then, after my first two children were born, I had a chance to tutor in a homeschool tutorial for 7th through 12th graders. A tutorial is a group setting where tutors are hired to teach classes in their areas of strength to groups of kids. They usually meet one or two days per week, and give children a chance to get together and socialize as well as learn difficult subjects.

I was impressed with how nice the kids were. I really wanted my children to turn out like the kids I was tutoring. They were happy and friendly, interested in learning, and were not particularly peer dependent. They were normal teens with a lot of friends, but there were some differences. They weren't intimidated by adults, and could play with small children without the scorn I had seen in other teens I had known. As a rule, they were confident and well grounded in who they were. I was hooked. I looked up the research available at that time (1993), talked with my husband, and we decided I would educate our children at home when they were old enough. In the meantime, I continued teaching classes at the tutorial.

However, I still had concerns. After all, most of the people I had grown up with were tied to professional education in some way. Homeschooling seemed so radical. So, I "tried it out" with my oldest daughter when she was 4 years old (before mandatory school age) just in case I found out that I didn't like it, or that I was really bad at it.

After 30 minutes a day (not always in one piece) doing 'school-ish' types of things and just learning to be aware of her academic needs, I found that she and I both were thriving. Her younger sister was also learning to love 'school time' with Mom. So, I made a commitment to homeschool the next year, and continued each year as long as it seemed to be working. During this time I had two more children, so I was learning to parent four children while teaching the two oldest.

The pregnancy with my fourth child was particularly draining, and I was regularly quizzed by friends and family members about my decision to homeschool. I was tired, and my two littlest ones were a handful, so I began to fantasize about all the time I would have if I only had two children to care for at home and didn't HAVE to teach the older two. I began to question our decision. Since the Kindergarten/First grade year did not go as well as the other two years, I began to wonder if I was really doing a good job. I also began to feel isolated because we didn't know many people in our community. Sending our girls to school began to look like the best solution. After visiting the local public school and talking with the great principal there, we decided to send our two older daughters to first and second grade the next year.

With great anticipation of the positive effects of school and the enthusiastic encouragement and support of close friends and family members (who were relieved that we were finally doing something 'normal'), we embarked upon that school adventure. Unfortunately, the principal we had talked to resigned and was replaced with someone who did not promote the type of school setting we were expecting. After two weeks in a great classroom with a wonderful teacher, my first-grade daughter was reassigned because of overcrowding, and the principal made it clear he would absolutely not consider parents' input in this process. Her new teacher was having a difficult year personally, and her style was not a good match for our daughter.

Then there were the simple realities of school. We sent our kids to school on the bus at 7:50 in the morning, and didn't see them again until after 4:00 in the afternoon. When they got home they wanted to run and play a little before settling down to do homework. I would help them with homework, sometimes a couple of hours of it, and then rush to get supper ready for the family. We would bathe the children, put them in bed, and start all over again the next morning.

We almost never had time to relax and talk with our children! This was a stark contrast to the family closeness we had had the year before. When we did get a chance to talk with them they told us about several assemblies that we were unaware of and that promoted social agendas. The school had not informed us of the content or that they would occur. I guess they just assumed that whatever they thought was best for our children would be fine with us. Often, they were wrong.

My daughters were academically advanced when they entered

school, but my six-year-old first-grade daughter still reversed a lot of her letters and numbers, and struggled considerably with writing. She could add, subtract, and multiply accurately, could read at a first grade level, and loved science, but unfortunately, all of these subjects in school were dependent on her ability to demonstrate her knowledge through her writing.

My happy, effervescent, self-confident and creative child started showing signs of significant stress, and basically stopped smiling. Her enthusiasm for learning plummeted. I tried to get involved, but found that any attempt to talk with the school system about her academics was seen as interference. I was labeled as the 'home-schooler.' As a certified teacher, it was frustrating to be told that I should leave the teaching to the 'professionals'.

We began to see behavior problems from her for the first time ever, and she did less and less of her seatwork each day. When she missed a day of school in November, she got make-up work from her teacher to complete over the Thanksgiving holidays. Work that the teacher thought was important enough to take several hours out of her vacation included cutting out pictures of pilgrims and coloring them according to a color chart, naming shapes, and identifying colors. She would have been able to do all of these assignments at the age of two. No wonder she didn't think her seatwork was important – it wasn't! It didn't seem right to waste her time in that way. So, she returned to homeschooling that November.

At the same time, my second-grade daughter was really enjoying school, so we left her in. We liked her teacher, and she seemed to be making friends. The only concern we had was that she became increasingly peer dependent. She was doing very well academically, so she was tested, and entered the gifted program. From the time we started that program, it struck me how much fun it was – and how much like our former homeschool. Unfortunately, she could only participate in this program for a half day each week, and was penalized if she did anything that took longer than the allotted time, even though it was a school activity.

For example, her gifted class went to see a play downtown, which was a 30-minute drive from her school. The play was long, and afterward there was less than one non-academic hour left at the end of the school day. Even if we had gone back to school immediately after the school sponsored activity, my daughter would have had a partial absence and make-up work. This was disheartening to a child who was trying to achieve perfect attendance. Most of the parents decided that they would do something special with their children to follow up on the lessons in the play. As expected, there were negative consequences. Although I don't begrudge the make-up work, or even a partial absence for keeping her out the rest of the day, it still was a punishment for following up on a wonderful learning experience.

Then, I began to realize the extent of control my daughter's peer group exerted over her. She was starting to be unkind and exclusive to kids outside of her clique, including her siblings, and was less and less responsive to me about it. I refused to accept this as 'normal,' and continued to work with her on this issue. When the group turned on her late in the year, she asked to return to homeschooling. Since it was close to the end of the year, we made her finish out the year and try to work out the problem with some help from us. It got a little better, but was never fully resolved. She began to realize her tendency to rely on peers for approval, and openly acknowledged, at the age of 7, that she didn't think she could stand up to that type of pressure long term.

So, I quit teaching classes at the tutorial, and returned to teaching all of my children at home. I discovered, to my surprise, that my daughters not only had not progressed much academically while in school, they had actually regressed in many areas. Things that they knew the year before they suddenly could no longer remember or do.

My first grade daughter, who had loved reading and was on the verge of bursting into advanced reading when I sent her to school, did not enjoy reading for at least a year after she stopped school. She also didn't show that sudden surge in reading ability that all the rest of my children experienced when at that stage.

My oldest daughter now did only what I asked of her, rather than exploring her interests to their fullest extent as she had before. In addition, she remembered very little of what she was taught in school. Even though she had gotten straight "A's," she really paid more attention to her friends than schoolwork.

The change in the quality of both of my daughters' academics was discouraging. They no longer saw education as part of their lifestyle, seamlessly integrated into their experiences. Instead, they saw it as a limited part of their lives, confined to certain hours of the day called 'school.' Those weren't even happy hours anymore. I was sad to see that happen. It took many years to regain a sense of interest in learning for its own sake, and it never returned to the level that existed before their formal school experience.

So, although many people are happy with their school experiences, school didn't work as well for us as home education. In spite of that, I am not against sending children to school. There are many wonderful schools out there, and many concerned, wonderfully involved parents send their children to them and are happy with the results. Good for them. They certainly have my blessing. They are taking responsibility for their children, and are raising them, utilizing school as a tool to meet their children's educational needs. I am glad schools exist for those who use them well.

I am, however, dismayed at the tendency of some parents to think that they no longer have control over, or responsibility for, their children's lives and educations. One of the most lasting impressions I will carry with me from that brief school experience is walking out of the school that first day and hearing several parents cheering, and one of them screaming, "I'm free!" amidst a round of laughter. They seemed to have surrendered their children completely to the care of the school, as if they were excited at the prospect of "free" childcare. That attitude has spilled beyond the school hours for many parents. I took exception to that attitude which, unfortunately, has its roots in the way parents are treated at some schools. Whether they accepted it or not, the responsibility to educate their children still rested squarely on their shoulders. As a former schoolteacher, I believe I can speak for most when I say that teachers are there to teach, not to baby-sit or raise the children in their care.

The year that we returned to home education I helped to get a homeschool support group going for local home educators and their children, and more or less shared some part in its administration for about four years. My children have participated in: Brownies, another homeschool group, baseball, softball, football, piano lessons, Vacation Bible School, Girls In Action and Royal Ambassadors (church groups on Wednesday nights), Bible Bowl, Children's School of Worship, community art classes, MATH-COUNTS (a national math competition program), and various field trips (some in groups, and some as a family). So, I understand the activity-led lives that many people get caught in, and my kids certainly have had a chance to 'socialize' with other kids.

Well, now I have an eighth grader, a seventh grader, a fourth grader, and a second grader (she skipped formal Kindergarten, which is a freedom more easily exercised in home education than at school). I have children who are gifted, ADHD, mildly seasonally hearing-impaired, auditory learners, visual learners, kinesthetic learners, musically-inclined, artistically inclined, right-brained, and left brained. Some of my children like math, some don't. Some like to write, some don't. I won't tell you which are which, although I do believe they are all gifted.

I have an assortment of learning styles and interests to keep me busy. The biggest blessing I experience from this is that I am able to adapt my teaching to accommodate their diverse styles and interests, and each child receives an education tailored to his or her needs. My oldest two children are now participating in the tutorial where I taught for so many years when they were young, and the other children are also involved in classes and social activities through that group. I am also tutoring there again. I'm enjoying this new era in our lives as we transition back to the tutorial where I first resolved to homeschool.

As you may have guessed, I like homeschooling. That's a good part of why I have continued to do it for so many years, and why I am writing this book. So, a lot of what I say in this book is pro-homeschooling. Although I have tried to include negatives where I find them, it is difficult to find much negative literature about home education that is based in research rather than opinion.

I also am a dedicated Christian. I have chosen not to make that a central theme of this book, simply because I know so many people who would not read it if it were filled with references to what I know to be the all-encompassing love and forgiveness of Jesus Christ. However, I am not ashamed of my beliefs, and I am sure they come out in what I write. I am not trying to hide what I believe; I am simply trying to make this book readable for those who have other beliefs, and for their family members and friends. Since I firmly believe that God is in control and I don't have to try to change lives for Him through my own actions, I leave that to

Him. I just want to be obedient, and I trust I have been in the way I have written this prayerfully-considered book.

Before the Questions—A Note For Home Educators:

People ask questions all the time when they don't really want to know the answers; they just seem to want evidence that their own choices were better, or they think they want to know until they hear your answers. Some people get very defensive of their own choices when they hear what others have opted to do, and a few of those get downright nasty. Others just want to be able to argue, and since home education is not as mainstream as other choices, that seems like a good place to start. So, here are some ways I answer questions in circumstances when the motive of the asker is not clear:

First and foremost, I give a short answer. This is best when you don't know why someone is asking. If they really want to hear more, they will probe more deeply. Here are some examples of a variety of possible responses to the question "So — WHY do you homeschool?"

- We enjoy it.
- It's best for us right now.
- It's best for a child we have right now because of a special need (the child is more advanced or is behind others in school in some area, or has behavioral or emotional issues that are better addressed at home, but this need not be said unless asked for).
- School didn't work for us.
- We're weird.
- We believe we are called to homeschool (a reply usually given in church to someone who understands that answer).
- We like homeschooling.
- We love seeing our children reach important milestones. We don't want to miss them.
- Because it's working well.
- We love what it gives us. What do you love about public/ private school?
- It's great to have a flexible schedule.

- We believe we are responsible for our children's education, and this is how we have chosen to take on that responsibility.
- We wanted to give them more opportunities than were available in school.
- We wanted our children to learn in the context of the real world, so they could use it when they're grown.
- We like our kids. We want to be with them.
- We want our children to be positively socialized.
- We can tailor the curriculum to meet the needs of our children.
- It fits our lifestyle.
- It allows us time to focus on (fill in the blank with whatever talent or ability your child has)
- No one's told us we can't!

These are just some examples of how this question can be answered in a short way for strangers who ask. It's best to try to have an honest, friendly approach, no matter how the question was asked.

WHY?

It's been a challenge to find a way to categorize questions and answers, but this is what I settled on: the rest of this book is divided into chapters and subsections phrased in question form. Most chapters have several 'questions' associated with them. The bold-faced questions may apply to many responses in the paragraphs that follow, so it is good to keep that in mind with the longer sections. Enjoy!

"So – WHY do you homeschool?"

Sometimes I find *myself* asking this question, even though I am very happy with our decision to homeschool our children. Homeschooling must seem truly overwhelming and strange for those who don't actually do it. This is the title question of the book, because it seems to be the one I hear the most often by strangers on the street (followed by its close second, "What about socialization?"). Every checkout person who has asked my kids why they weren't in school has either followed up by asking this or has wanted to. So, I am answering this one up front, once and for all, or at least until the next time I shop during the day!

There are as many reasons for homeschooling as there are homeschoolers, but since it is so fundamental, most researchers have asked it, and every article references it. A lot of people assume that most people homeschool to avoid public schools, but that's not the only reason. Many parents would educate their own children even if they lived in the top-performing school district in the nation. Often, the choice has more to do with a preference for what home-schooling has to offer than a distaste for schools. With that in mind, I will begin this chapter with reasons that reflect that preference.

However, dissatisfaction with schools can certainly be a factor. If there were no problems in the available schools, many of us may not have thought to take it upon ourselves to do what we do. Also, school concerns have been cited as the main reason for home-schooling in recent surveys by the U. S. Department of Education.[1] Many of the other reasons why parents choose to educate their children at home can be related to this one. So, I will finish this section with a discussion of what, specifically, bothers some parents enough about schools to remove their children from them.

Some homeschool because...

...parents want more, and more relaxed, family time.

In our current educational system, children are generally sent away from the home at the tender age of five, if not earlier, and spend about seven hours each day away from home. This does not include the hour or so of bus time, or before-and-after school care for hard-working parents. These hours are the prime time of the day for inter-acting. Then, children may spend one to four hours or more on homework a day (depending on age and other factors), and increasingly will be involved in at least one extracurricular activity per week.

Between chores, meals, baths, and the other requirements of daily life, children don't get much of a chance to talk with their parents on a personal and relaxed level. After thirteen or more years of this, it is no wonder that many parents have lost a level of intimacy with their children. Most parents want to be the major influence in their children's lives. Most children want that, too. Unfortunately, the major part of kids' lives is spent away from their parents when they go to school, and what's left is often controlled by school directives such as homework, fundraisers, parent-teacher meetings, extracurricular activities, etc. It's not surprising that over time children stop relating to their parents as the primary influences in their lives.

Homeschoolers, by contrast, can manage their own schedules, and thus can include 'down' time for everyone in the family. We can have regular, intimate family activities and just enjoy one another. We don't have to choose between time together and school, so we can keep close relationships in the family. This is one of the greatest joys of homeschooling.

There are other benefits to being more involved as a family, too. Parental involvement in education is a consistently cited factor in the educational attainment and the well-being of children. According the National Middle School Association (NMSA), "Parent involvement has been linked with student outcomes including increased achievement test results, a decrease in dropout rate, improved attendance, improved student behavior, higher grades, higher grade point average, greater commitment to schoolwork, and improved attitude toward school."[2] These factors are often repeated in research. Home education is simply the epitome of parent involvement.

...parents want to pass on their own values to their children.

Everything is so much more confusing than it once was. People in our society once agreed on the basics of what was right and what was wrong, at least publicly, and made an effort to help others stay within the boundaries of what was right. Parents helped each other to reinforce society's values in the children they knew. Now everyone is afraid to correct anyone else's children because the standards can't be agreed upon anymore.

James Dobson wrote something in his book <u>Bringing Up Boys</u>[3] that really stuck with me: Parents in the past were under a lot of pressure to support societal values, and were considered bad parents if they counteracted cultural norms. Parents today are considered bad parents if they do NOT counteract cultural norms. We can't just rely on following the rules anymore; we have to sift through each decision and figure out what we value and what we don't.

Many schools have tried to set a standard by teaching values to the children in their care. No longer are children simply being exposed to different values while at school; they are systematically being taught values chosen by the schools. Since schools have entered into this business with programs like 'values clarification' and 'death education', many of us have begun asking ourselves if the values taught in school are the ones we want our children to have. Often, they are not. By making a way to spend more time with our children, we can take a larger part in passing on values we believe will better equip our children for their adult lives.

...parents want to teach their children from their religious viewpoint.

It is clear that schools are much less supportive of the religious values and beliefs of their students than they once were. According to a report described in the News Telegraph, education ministers in the United Kingdom believe children "should...be told *from an early age* [emphasis mine] of the alternatives to marriage and that there are non-religious ways of marking momentous experiences." The report included this statement: "Pupils would be actively encouraged to question the religious beliefs they bring with them into the classroom, not so they are better able to defend or rationalise them, but so they are genuinely free to adopt whatever position on religious matters they judge to be best supported by the evidence."[4] This official document discussed practices for children from the age of five and up.

Although this ministry is in the United Kingdom, the opinions expressed are similar to those in many intellectual educational circles in the United States. Unfortunately, those circles often control or influence school policies.[5] I think that the age of five is a little young for children to "adopt whatever position on religious matters they judge to be best supported by the evidence." I also doubt the objectivity of the 'evidence' presented in many school systems.

Christians are not the only ones who feel it is important to pass on religious values in everyday life. Muslims are a fast-growing portion of the homeschool community, too. Many activities engaged in at public schools make it difficult to practice Islam in a sincere way. The same is true for Orthodox Judaism, Hinduism, and many other religions represented in our society.

Schools may cry "tolerance" very loudly, but in practice many would be happiest if we 'religionists' just kept all religious observances to ourselves. While some teachers truly wish to broaden the experiences of students by exposing them to a wide variety of religious beliefs, they often do it in ways that violate the creeds of members of other religious beliefs. In attempting to value aspects of all religious creeds, schools in actuality manage to offend the beliefs of all except those who hold no deep religious beliefs at all. It is no surprise that parents with strong religious convictions object to this.

...parents are called to homeschool by God

Being called to homeschool is different from just wanting to teach your religion to your children. One is highly personal and relational, while the other is just imparting information. So, what exactly IS a calling from God? Well, first of all, it's NOT proof that someone is crazy. Callings have been a part of Christian living since Adam named the animals, and they're very real. A calling is simply a unique and specific directive given by God for a specific purpose.

Sometimes He directs you to do something at a specific time, like being called to serve as a deacon in a church. Sometimes a calling sets the direction for your entire life, like a calling to take care of the poor or to the medical profession. Always, though, a calling affects your life and your relationship with God.

So — how do people know if they are being called to do something by God? There are many different ways God can speak to you. Sometimes He makes what you are reading in the Bible stand out in such a strong way that you *know* He is speaking to you. I guess you could say that you know in your "knower." Other times, He confirms and reconfirms what He wants to say to you through circumstances in your life. Or, He may answer a prayer in such a miraculous and specific way that you know He is directing you.

Of course, God is very creative, and won't be put in a box. As soon as we say He will do something one way, He surprises us with something new. That's the way He is! It's never boring when you truly listen to God and follow Him. But, when the Creator of the whole universe tells you to act, it's a good idea to respond and obey. Obedience to God's calling is a very serious thing.[6] And, if God calls you to do something, He will give you the strength to do it.[7] This is both my belief and my experience. Many Christians believe that God has directed them to educate their children themselves.

...parents want the most personalized and best educational option for their children

Individualization is as important for educating children as choosing well-fitting clothes is for dressing them. The difference between home education and classroom schooling is like the difference between hiring a tailor and telling someone to go buy clothes for an 'average' eight-year-old child. The chances are good that the buyer will miss the target in some way, while the tailor will produce well-fitting clothes designed just for that child. Eight year olds come in all shapes and sizes, and have many different ideas about what clothes would be best for them. The same is true of curricula and learning styles.

In a classroom, there is one text or method chosen for a subject. Changing the text often requires applying to a committee, and is a long and complicated process. A really good teacher will use several different styles to reach as many children as possible most of the time, but still has to use the same text for the whole class, and one program can never reach all the children all the time.

Parents, who know their own children well, can tailor an educational experience to fit each child's personality, learning style, strengths, weaknesses, and preferences. In a one-on-one tutoring situation, it is possible to change your teaching and materials to meet the needs of each child each time. If you make a mistake, you can correct it as soon as it is discovered. You can try as many methods as needed to find a perfect fit, and consult an unlimited number of experts to find something that works. This results in superior learning for your child, usually in less time, as well as a greater bonding experience between you and your child.

... dissatisfaction with the local public and private schools

It is important to note that most home educating parents don't have a problem with most *teachers* in schools. We pretty much agree that most schoolteachers are dedicated professionals who enter the teaching profession because they love children. In fact, many of us ARE schoolteachers. One study estimated that one-fourth of homeschooled children have at least one certified teacher for a parent.[8] It is not the teachers that are the problem most of the time; it is the schools, their bureaucracies, their methodology, and the political machine that runs them that make some schools intolerable. Of course, some teachers clearly *are* a problem, at least for specific children. Because this section is so long, I'll break it up into smaller pieces to pinpoint specific problems.

Some parents are dissatisfied with local school choices because...

...the schools aren't working for their children.
It's a terrible thing to watch your child flounder, and a worse one to feel powerless to help him do his best within the system. When your child isn't progressing satisfactorily, it's only natural to want to take action. This is true for parents of accelerated and struggling students alike.

I know many dedicated, involved parents who have tried to work out problems within the school system, but who felt they were pushed away by overwhelmed, disorganized, or controlling teachers and/or administrators. It was fine for them to bring brownies on party days, to raise money for the renovation of the cafeteria, or to do odd jobs requested by the teacher, but it was definitely NOT ok to question teaching methods or practices, or to suggest alternatives for a child who wasn't doing well. Even if suggestions were taken, they may have been implemented in a haphazard way or were embarrassing to the child. This is devastating for parents who know a situation is not working for their child, but can't find a way to get involved effectively.

These are the parents who often pull a child out of school in the middle of the year, and only homeschool one of their children. The intention is usually to put a child back together and/or just to get her though the school year. Some parents do just that, but many of these parents (in my experience) often continue homeschooling the next year, and end up educating all their children at home before they are done.

...the school's expectations are too low.

It's really hard to teach the number and variety of children who are in the modern school systems. Some kids come to school totally unprepared for the social and intellectual demands of school life. Schools trying to meet the needs of these special children sometimes make *all* children march through the basics to make sure *all* children are ready for more difficult work.

Well, some children *do* enter school ready to learn, and the basics are not appropriate for them. It's frustrating to wait a year or two for other kids to catch up before the school begins to present appropriate challenges for *your* child. Low expectations are not helpful to anyone and result in many bright kids losing interest in school.

This is especially true for many minority families at this point in history. Schools can try so hard to 'accommodate' different cultural backgrounds that they don't hold *all* children to the same high standard of academics. This is certainly one reason why committed African-American parents are turning to homeschooling in record numbers. They find that the bright, interested kindergarteners they sent to school are coming home to them as rebellious, frustrated fourth graders who struggle to keep up academically with their peers.

However, low expectations are not limited to minority children, nor are they limited to the academics at school. All children will test behavioral expectations under the right circumstances. Most parents want their children and their children's peers to be held accountable for their behavior. What they see in some schools, however, is that problem behavior is not confronted until it hits a crisis point. The result? Crisis situations are the rule rather than the exception in those schools.

...the behavior problems in some schools are significant.

Behavior problems in some schools are overwhelming. More children are victims of bullying, and many schoolchildren witness grossly inappropriate behavior on the part of their schoolmates regularly. According to *Indicators of School Crime and Safety: 2003* : "School violence can make students fearful and affect their readiness and ability to learn."[9] Teachers and administrators are dealing with serious behavior problems they wouldn't have seen a generation ago. It can really wear teachers and non-violent students down.

Because of this, smaller misbehaviors may not be addressed, so some children begin to think they are okay. At least they realize that they can get away with 'smaller' behavior problems. That's almost worse than not knowing the difference between right and wrong, because it opens the door to testing every limit to see what is defined as 'small.' Children have to figure out what's right or wrong in each situation, and that's not going to yield positive results. They also learn that some rules aren't really important because they are rarely enforced.

In some schools, principals and teachers make the mistake of focusing on those who misbehave. This gives all the attention to the children with problems, thus slighting those who are doing the right thing. It's troubling to send a well-behaved child to school and watch good behavior erode, and sometimes get mocked, by peers. It's worse to then find that your well-behaved child gets none of the teacher's attention while troublemakers consume her time. Even when good behavior is noticed by the teachers, that alone is sometimes enough to expose a child to ridicule from peers. It can be a vicious cycle. Behavior in these schools just seems to get worse and worse. Children are unrealistically and negatively 'socialized' in these situations.

...safety is an issue in school.

School is less safe than it once was. Here are a few incidents of school violence reported since 1996, according to a 2001 World Magazine article: "Barry Loukaitis, 14, shoots up his algebra class in Moses Lake, Wash., killing the teacher and two students. It's the first in what will seem an uninterrupted string of school shootings. Next will come Bethel, Alaska (a principal and one student killed); then Pearl, Miss. (two students killed, seven wounded); West Paducah, Ky. (three students killed, five wounded while praying); Jonesboro, Ark. (four students and one teacher killed, 10 others wounded); Edinboro, Pa. (one teacher killed, two students wounded); and Springfield, Ore. (two students killed and 22 wounded). These will seem dwarfed by the carnage at Columbine High School in Littleton, Colo., when on April 20, 1999, 14 students and a teacher will be killed, along with 23 others wounded."[10]

According to the "Indicators of School Crime and Safety:

2003"[11] report:

- "In all survey years from 1993 to 2001, between 7 percent and 9 percent of students [in grades 9-12] reported being threatened or injured with a weapon, such as a gun, knife, or club, on school property" (p. 12).
- "Seventy-one percent of public schools experienced one or more violent incidents, while 36 percent reported one or more such incidents to the police" (p. 20).
- "In both 1999 and 2001, students were more likely to be afraid of being attacked at school or on the way to and from school than away from school." (p. 36)
- "In 1999-2000, more than one-quarter (29 percent) of public schools reported daily or weekly student bullying" (p. 16).
- This was followed up immediately with the statement, "Discipline problems in a school may contribute to an overall environment in which violence and crime may occur" (p. 16).

Quite simply, school violence has some parents really spooked. School massacres that have made the news are still fresh in the minds of a number of parents, but that's not the only kind of violence that takes place there. Those incidents just spotlighted the everyday violence that takes place in many schools. There are tragic and long-term affects associated with bullying. Suicides, mental illnesses and disorders, murders, school shootings, and other anti-social and criminal behaviors are linked with ongoing bullying.[12] Even if children are not victims of harassment or a crime in school, they seem quite likely to witness that behavior there. Emotional and spiritual safety, as well as physical safety, are in jeopardy when children are in constant contact with situations that are dangerous or anti-social.

...academics are not as important to the school as the social agenda.

Why do we send our children to school? To learn, of course! It's not unreasonable to want academics to be the primary concern of public schools. Unfortunately, some schools spend more time engaged in social engineering than teaching plain old reading, writing, and arithmetic — the skills children will need to prepare them for college and employment in the future.

Between drug awareness campaigns, death education, values clarification, tolerance training, sex education (including 'alternative' sex education), visits from local political leaders, fun day on Friday, etc., teachers in some schools can't promote a consistent, demanding course of academics. It is especially frustrating to see academics pushed aside for social agendas that conflict with a family's personal belief system. Some of us just want schools to teach our children to read, write, and do math well. When they don't, we take matters into our own hands.

...they disagree with the goals and purposes of the education unions that set the policies of the public schools.

Some of the annual resolutions of the National Education Association (NEA), one of the most powerful teacher's unions and lobbying agencies in the nation, are shocking. I first became aware of them when there was a brief public outcry after they were widely circulated on the Internet in 1999. Since then, the NEA has continued to make annual resolutions that fly in the face of mainstream American morality. The union often receives little or no public attention for them, though, perhaps because the NEA makes it very difficult for the average parent to find out exactly what they say at those annual meetings. I read some of the 2004 resolutions on the Eagle Forum website because direct searches for the resolutions on the NEA website were unproductive.[13]

The 2004 resolutions included an astonishing number of references to sexual topics for our children, including sexual orientation, gender identification, gays, lesbians, bisexuals, transgendered people, and homophobia, often then described using the general term 'diversity.' The NEA supported using recruitment, hiring and promotion practices, textbook revisions, curricula, programs, and instructional and resource materials, and other methods that would "Increase respect, understanding, acceptance, and sensitivity toward individuals and groups in a diverse society...", and specifically listed a number of different sexually defined groups to promote in schools.[14] The number and variety of resolutions devoted to sexual orientation and related topics make it clear that the NEA was not discussing fighting discrimination, as implied; instead, this powerful education union was talking about promoting deviant sexual behavior as normal and positive. This is unacceptable to the majority of parents who send their children to school, but most parents are unaware of the goals or power of this huge education group.

The number of controversial issues addressed was incredible, especially if you wade through the wording, go a little deeper and realize what is really being said. For example, the NEA "supports family planning, including the right to reproductive freedom."[15] Family planning and reproductive freedom? For largely unmarried, minor teens and younger students? This is just politically correct speech for teaching children how to avoid having babies when they have sex (family planning) and how to abort babies when they do, inconveniently, intrude upon their lives (reproductive freedom).

Sexual topics, though prevalent in the resolutions, are not the only controversial ones. The NEA does not believe in using competency testing to weed out teachers who don't know their subjects. It supports early education for children from birth through age eight at a time when others are questioning the wisdom of sending children away from the family as early as we currently do.[16] The resolutions consistently support global authority rather than national authority over our country.[17]

Of course, the NEA doesn't think much of home education, either. The group asserts that all home educators must be licensed teachers and use only state-sponsored curriculum, but should not be allowed to participate in any activities (like athletics) sponsored by the schools.[18] If we did that, that would negate many positive aspects of homeschooling, and we might as well send our children to school. I guess that's what the union hopes.

Despite all the rhetoric about 'tolerance' and 'diversity,' the NEA displays a remarkable intolerance toward those who choose to educate their children differently. The NEA opposes any competition. This is clear when the resolutions are taken as a whole, and even in some specific resolutions. Here's one good example: "The National Education Association condemns the philosophy and practices of extremist groups and urges active opposition to all such movements that are inimical to the ideals of the Association."[19] In the collective mind of the union, any group or movement that opposes the NEA is extremist. In my mind, however, the *NEA* is the extremist group, and its philosophy and practices are inimical (hostile) to my ideals. Some of us are simply too stubborn to accept the agenda of the teachers' unions as our own.

These resolutions were written by a wealthy union with armies of lobbyists and lots of power. Every year it uses its political weight to increase the visibility of its agendas in our schools, and its influence is increasingly felt. Laws are written to increase control, textbooks are adapted to match its values, and teacher hiring practices are changed to ensure that those altered textbooks get used.

The NEA does get one thing right, though. An article on the NEA website strongly encourages parents to be involved in their children's educations. In fact, the article gives a few telling bits of information: "In study after study, researchers discover how important it is for parents to be actively involved in their child's education." "A home environment that encourages learning is more important to student achievement than income, education level or cultural background." "Three kinds of parental involvement at home are consistently associated with higher student achievement: actively organizing and monitoring a child's time, helping with homework and discussing school matters."[20] I agree with all these statements. This involvement is much easier to implement in a home setting than in an institutional one.

"Why not just send them to private schools, if you don't like the public ones?"

Private schools are often a starting point in the thought process for families considering an alternative to public schools. They are often really expensive, though, and many families would have to seriously change their lifestyles in order to afford them if they could manage the payments at all.

The cost is not the only stumbling block, however. Some of the same disadvantages of public schools are also evident in private ones. Some examples: 1. Group schooling is constructed for the convenience of the school, rather than its effectiveness in teaching children. Individual tutoring is much more effective academically. 2. When children are put in a situation where the ratio of kids to adults is 15:1 or more, they tend to get more social input from their peers than from adults. That means they are learning the 'right' way to act from children with no more social experience than they have. 3. Sending children to school still means giving up the biggest and best portion of their days to someone else.

Thus, there are reasons other than finances that steer some families away from local private schools. Also, there are many, many more reasons people choose to teach their children at home than just dissatisfaction with public schools.

"Why not send them to religious schools, if you homeschool for religious reasons?"

Religion is highly personal, and it is difficult to pass something that personal to a child in a group setting. It is also difficult to find a school that believes exactly as you do. Even the best religious schools have chosen a doctrine to follow. While that doctrine may be closer to what you believe than the humanist doctrines in secular schools, it will still not match you perfectly.

In the most extreme cases, if you leave the teaching of religion to schools, that's all you will get. What I mean by that is that children will learn about *religion* at school but not about a *relationship* with God. This is comparable to learning *about* your father, but never actually meeting him personally. What a bummer.

While many parents do an excellent job of teaching their children what they believe after school, it's just easier to teach them when you are the major influence in their lives, rather than the second major influence. In addition, Christian home educators are sometimes following a mandate that instructs them to teach their own children at every opportunity during daily activities.[21] That is something they can only do when their children are available to them during daily activities. Of course, the problems with other types of private schools and public schools come into play here, too, like avoiding expensive tuition payments and the reduced effectiveness of group instruction.

Endnotes for chapter 2:

1. National Center for Education Statistics surveys in 1999 and in 2003 by

Stacey Bielick and associates.

2. Kettler, R., and Valentine, J. (2000). *NMSA Research Summary # 18: Parent Involvement and Student Achievement at the Middle Level (2000)*. National Middle School Association. Retrieved June 16, 2005, from http://www.nmsa.org/research/ressum18.htm

3. James Dobson is founder of Focus on the Family. Bringing Up Boys can be ordered from the Focus on the Family website at http://www.family. org/resources/itempg.cfm?itemid=5083

4. This report is titled, *"What is Religious Education For?"* and was described in an article by Melissa Kite in a February 15, 2004, article in the News.Telegraph called *Children should learn more about atheism and less about Jesus, says Labour think-tank.*

5. One good source for the National Education Association's (NEA) resolutions is the Eagle Forum website at http://www.eagleforum.org /educate/2004/aug04/NEA-resolutions.html. For American Federation of Teachers (AFT) resolutions, go to http://www.aft.org. It has a searchable website, and the word 'resolution' will turn up pages related to each of the AFT's resolutions.

6. 1 Corinthians 1:24-31, Romans 11:29, Ephesians 1:15-19a, Ephesians 4:1-7, 2 Thessalonians 1:11-12.

7. Exodus 3:10-22, Jeremiah 1:5-8.

8. From Lawrence Rudner's 1999 study, *Scholastic Achievement and Demographic Characteristics of Home School Students in 1998* available to view at http://www.hslda.org/docs/study/rudner1999/FullText. asp

9. From page 36 of *Indicators of School Crime and Safety: 2003* by Devoe, et al. (2003).

10. From *History 101,* the cover story of the April 28, 2001 issue of World Magazine.

11. This 2003 report was put out by joint efforts of the National Center for Education Statistics (NCES) and the Bureau of Justice Statistics (BJS) and was authored by Devoe et al.

12. Starr, L. (2000, July 11). *Sticks and Stones and Names Can Hurt You: De-Myth-tifying the Classroom Bully!* Education World. Retrieved July 27, 2005 from http://www.education-world.com/a_issues/issues102. shtml

13. One good source for the NEA resolutions is the Eagle Forum website at http://www.eagleforum.org/educate/2004/aug04/NEA-resolutions.html. For AFT (American Federation of Teachers) resolutions, go to http://www.aft.org. It has a searchable website, and the word "resolution" will turn up pages related to each of the AFT's resolutions.

14. Resolutions B-7, B-9, B-31, B-39, B-40, C-28, D-8, F-1, and I-39. All resolutions cited are from the annual meeting in 2004.

15. Resolution I-12.

16. Resolutions D-21 and B-1; Raymond Moore has written numerous

books, including <u>School Can Wait</u>, that enumerate the problems of sending children away from parents at an early age.
17. Resolutions I-1, I-2, And I-47.
18. Resolution B-69.
19. Resolution C-15.
20. This article is called *Getting Involved in Your Child's Education*, and is available at <u>http://www.nea.org/parents/index.html</u>.
21. Deuteronomy 6:9 is one example.

Who Homeschools?

"What is a *typical* homeschooler like, anyway?"

Homeschoolers tend to be politically conservative, except when they are liberal, and are religious, except when they are not. Confused? Well, you're in good company. Many attempts have been made to figure out what the typical home educator is like, and each time there have been serious problems with the results. Sometimes only one kind of homeschooler is asked to respond to a survey, and that creates a bias. Many home educators don't like to respond to invasive questionnaires, so that keeps them from being included in survey results.

There are a few things that researchers have determined, however, although they don't all agree. Home educators tend to have gone farther in school than average parents, have more children than most American families, and are more likely to remain in two-parent households with only one of the parents working full-time. Some studies have described us as more religious and slightly more 'white' than average. [1]

However, that just describes the *average*. When you are averaging numbers, it doesn't make any difference whether 150 is the average of 1 and 299, or of 149 and 151. Sometimes the numbers are close to the average, and sometimes they aren't. When you are talking about people, it's important to remember that the average doesn't necessarily describe the individuals in the group. That's the case with home educators. In reality, we can be rich or poor, religious or atheistic, young or old, politically liberal or conservative. Home educators make up an incredibly diverse crowd. We're pretty individualistic, too, so it's hard to define us as a group.

If I had to come up with one characteristic that seems to define us, though, I'd have to say that it's dedication to our children. We don't have a typical 'look', or a standard way of speaking, but we are all trying to look out for the interests of our children in a direct, involved way. So I guess we have a lot in common with many parents who don't homeschool.

"Isn't it just the religious nuts who homeschool?"

Define "nut" (grin). The short answer to this question is "no." While religion plays a part in the choice to home educate for many families, most families who teach their children at home make the choice for a variety of reasons. In a 1999 Department of Education survey, 48.9 percent of parents selected "Can give child better education at home" as *one* of their reasons for homeschooling, while only 38.4 percent selected "Religious reasons."[2] In the 2003 version of the survey, 31 percent of families listed "concern about environment of other schools" as their *main* reason to homeschool, although that was closely followed by the 30 percent who chose "to provide religious or moral instruction."[3]

Thus, in 1999 less than two out of five chose 'religious reasons' as even one reason for their decision to teach their children at home, and one-and-a-half out of five chose religion as the main reason in 2003. So, the image that 'only religious people homeschool' is not accurate. Some of this bias is based on earlier research about home education that only surveyed people from certain religious groups. This prevented non-religious people from being part of the studies. Although much of the momentum in the current home education movement is fueled by Christian homeschoolers, there are many home educators who don't fit the religious mold.

"How many homeschoolers are there in the United States, anyway?"

It's hard to estimate the number of homeschoolers in the United

States for a variety of reasons. The first problem has to do with the definition of homeschooling. Many students are educated at home for short periods of time and for lots of reasons, including illness, delinquent behavior, etc. I am only going to focus on families that home educate by choice when other options are available to them.

Also, states have different reporting requirements for home education. Homeschools may be defined as private schools in some states, for example, which makes homeschoolers hard to distinguish from private school students. Also, since some home educators are reluctant to be counted, numbers are often 'weighted' to eliminate possible sources of error. This weighting can sometimes reflect researcher bias.

In spite of all that, many attempts have been made to estimate the number of home educated students over the last decade or so. Government agencies[4] have made some attempts that are worth looking at, even though they acknowledge that there are many sources of mistakes.[5] Here are some of the government-sponsored numbers that have been published, placed in historical order so you can see how the numbers have changed over time:

- According to a 1999 online paper called *Homeschoolers: Estimating Numbers and Growth* by Patricia Lines, "Growth has persisted over three decades. Earlier estimates, based on different methodologies, suggested 60,000 to 125,000 school-aged children for the fall of 1983; and 122,000 to 244,000 for fall of 1985; between 150,000 to 300,000 for fall of 1988; and between 250,000 to 350,000 for fall of 1990. A retroactive estimate done in 1988 suggested 10,000 to 15,000 children received their education at home in the late 1970s and early 1980s, close to an estimate made at the time by an early leader of the homeschooling movement, educator and author, John Holt" (p. 4).

- In 1994, the Census Bureau estimated that about 345,000 school-aged children in the United States were home-schooled.[6] That translated to about 0.8 percent of the school-aged population at that time.

- The U. S. Department of Education (USDE) estimated there were about 636,000 homeschooled children in 1996, or approximately1.4 percent of the school-aged population[7]. That represents a 26 percent increase over the previous estimate in 1994.

- In 2001, the USDE published another estimate, and came up with the figure of 850,000 children in 1999.[8] This reflected about 1.9 percent of the population and is a 33.6 percent increase over the survey's 1996 number.

- The latest USDE estimate was in 2003, indicating that there were about 1.1 million homeschooled children in the United States.[9] That's about 2.2 percent of the roughly 50 million school-aged children in the nation in 2003, and represents a 29 percent increase in homeschoolers since the previous estimate in 1999.

Although there has been concern after each count that perhaps the number of homeschoolers has been overestimated, and that the growth of home education may be exaggerated, increases have been pretty steady in official counts. If anything, official growth has slowed down – especially after 'error' has been accounted for and reduced by weighting the counts according to census estimates.

Government depictions of homeschooling tend to be limited, and often prefer data that favor public schooling. Most of these estimates contain language expressing doubts that there are really that many children taught at home. These issues make me doubt that they are sufficient estimates. Even so, official counts show a continuous growth in homeschooling from one estimate to the next.

Those are the official, government-sponsored numbers. It's interesting to compare these to homeschool-friendly counts made by those who are directly involved with home educators. So, here are some numbers put forth by homeschool advocates:

- According to a study published in 1997 by Dr. Brian D. Ray,[10] there were between 1,103,000 and 1,348,000 home-educated students in 1996. That's about double what the USDE estimated at that time, and represented about 2.4 percent to 2.9 percent of the population of school-aged children.

- According to the Home School Legal Defense Association (HSLDA) website, hslda.org, "An estimated 250,000 to 340,000 high school (grades 9-12) students were being home schooled during the 2000-2001 conventional school year."[11]

- Also according to the HSLDA website, Dr. Ray's 2002-2003 estimate is more accurate than the official estimates, with estimates of 1.7 to 2.1 million homeschoolers.[12] That would indicate that about 3.4 percent to 4.2 percent of the school-aged population is homeschooled.

Clearly, homeschool advocates think there are more home educators than the government does. I suspect that the reality is somewhere in the middle, with a current total of between 1.1 and 2.1 million (about 2.2 to 4.2 percent) school-age students educated at home. To put it another way, somewhere between one out of every fifty and one out of every twenty-five students in this country is home educated.

Just for comparison, private schools enrolled about 5.3 million students in 2001-2002, while public schools were projected to have enrolled about 48.3 million in 2004, according to the U. S. Department of Education.[13] While home education is not one of the top educational choices, it's not exactly rare, either.

According to comments from local support group leaders across the country, the growth of these groups is notable and continuous. For example, a new homeschool group formed in 2004 as the fifth such group in a small community near where I live. At the beginning of the opening year, 60 families were involved. By the end of that year, that number had grown to 85. 125 families signed up to participate in 2005, which accounts for 500 members, including parents and students. This is not an uncommon report. So, whatever the exact number is, there are a lot of homeschoolers, and both homeschooling and public education sources agree that the number is increasing each year.

What has contributed to this growth? Well, see the section on "Why do you homeschool?" in chapter two. However, charges to remove Christian children from the public schools by religious groups, most notably Focus on the Family and some Southern Baptists,[14] probably have contributed to some of the most recent growth. The fact that home education is becoming more visible in everyday life also makes a big difference. Most people know parents who teach their own children now, and can judge the effectiveness of it for themselves. In addition, the abundance of available support, both in the form of materials and real people who home educate, has made the choice easier in recent years than ever before.

"What about minorities?"

African-Americans:

African-Americans are a large minority segment of the homeschooling community, and the number of black home educators is growing exponentially. According to a May, 2003 article by Fox News, "black children are now (sic) five times more likely to be home schooled than five years ago."[15] Although the visibility of African-American home educators has been small across the short recorded history of the modern homeschool movement, it is increasing at an amazing rate. There is a growing number of websites dedicated to supporting this portion of the movement.

The parents I know who teach children of color at home give a number of reasons for homeschooling, but the most common I hear among my friends and in the media is that minority parents are fed up with low expectations and poor behavioral standards for their children. All Americans want their children to be able to do whatever they are capable of doing, without artificial hindrances. A culture of low expectations is one of the most devastating handicaps possible, and it is preventable. No parents want their children subjected to low expectations over a long period of time.

Unfortunately, some schools have lower expectations for minority students than they do for others. According to an article on A To Z's Home's Cool website, "Minorities battle subtle forms of racism every day in public schools (Sarver, 2003), so it would be no surprise that the reason so many minorities are leaving public education may have to do with an attempt to escape the passive forms of institutional racism they are subjected to (Boyden, Johnson, and Pittz, 2001)."[16]

""Families are running out of options," said Jennifer James, founder of the National African-American Homeschoolers Alliance, a non-religious organization based in North Carolina. "There's this persistent achievement gap, and a lot of black children are doing so poorly in traditional schools that parents are looking for alternatives.""[17] The achievement gap which is so enduring in public schools was largely absent or greatly reduced in at least one study of homeschoolers.[18] This is attractive to committed parents looking for solutions to these long-standing issues.

Also, most discerning parents want their kids to associate with children whose parents have high behavioral standards for them, which is not always the case in school settings. In some places, cultural and peer support requiring responsible behavior from young black men is lacking. This is not the case in the home education community, and the African-American parents I know who homeschool find like-minded parents who are raising responsible peers for their children.

African-Americans at this point in history are battling issues from a number of sources, and need stable families to succeed. The strong emphasis on family life in home education is an attraction for minorities who are surrounded by single parent households. Rebuilding a culture that supports stable families is not easy, and many black families are finding more success in the homeschool arena than in public school settings.

Muslims:

Muslims are a significant portion of the American homeschooling population. In fact, in 2001 Patrick Basham cites several sources to make the statement that "Muslim Americans … are the fastest growing sub-group within the home schooling movement. The number of home schooled Muslim Americans is predicted to double every year for the next eight years."[19] There are many websites emerging to support this population of home educators.

Of course, Muslim home educators have a lot in common with other homeschoolers, and can use many of the same resources. In the individualism of homeschooling, Muslim children can reach their potential without being forced to violate their principles. Muslims parents who are open to interacting with people of other faiths will also find a warm and supportive community of concerned parents with whom to share their burdens.

Other minority populations:

There are many other subgroups within the home education community that are often under-reported and overlooked by the mainstream media. Some of those are religious minorities, including Pagans, Buddhists, Hindus, and members of other world religions. Some are ethnic and cultural minorities in the United States, including Asians, Latinos, immigrants from a number of countries, and the subgroups within them. There are home educators from almost all minority groups in the United States, and online communities are forming to support these subgroups. If there are no existing support systems available in the community, an Internet search will probably turn up like-minded homeschoolers pretty quickly. Most homeschoolers are very helpful and are willing to help provide support for others, regardless of their backgrounds.

Racism:

Homeschoolers are sometimes accused of teaching their children at home to segregate their children from other races or religions. That is not the case in the groups I am a part of. Most homeschoolers I know want their children to come into contact with well-behaved children from a number of backgrounds, and often consciously and actively seek out others from different backgrounds.

I once had someone accuse me of keeping my children at home so that I could prevent them from having contact with minority students. The exact opposite is true. I want my children to get to know people from all backgrounds and ethnic groups. I just don't want my children to form opinions of others *based upon* their racial makeup. The racism I see in the local schools in the form of low expectations and academic and behavioral double standards sends a message to children that I don't want mine to receive.

In an attempt to honor racial diversity, some schools deliberately and regularly highlight the differences between children based on their racial, ethnic, and cultural backgrounds. This causes children to separate themselves into their own groups, and promotes a double standard that accentuates the differences between groups rather than unifying them. Racial issues are constantly monitored and special rules are made to avoid situations that *might* happen. This is not helpful. It reinforces racial and ethnic cliques, and promotes silent stereotyping, judgment, and resentment. It's better just to stick to a reasonable standard for everyone, even if it is not the mythical 'universal' standard.

I am delighted that my children associate with children from a variety of ethnic groups who are basically well-behaved, academically and intellectually challenged, and interested in learning. There is no artificial line separating children on the basis of their ethnicity. These children, by the way, attend public, private, and home schools. They are simply the cream of the crop from all the school options, and encourage responsible behavior in my own children. Giving my children an opportunity to interact positively with children from a wide variety of different racial and ethnic backgrounds is a strong attraction to home education for me.

Cultural and ethnic diversity CAN be celebrated without maintaining a double standard for excellence. Racial motivation is a great reason to homeschool, as the subculture that promotes ethnic separation in the schools is absent in the individualism of the home educating community. We are already separate entities. We don't spend our lives being identified as a group, so we already expect each person and each family to be different. People tend to be judged individually, more by the content of their character than the color of their skin. That is a type of unity I approve of, based on the words of Dr. Martin Luther King, Jr. — a man whose high standards and courageous actions I admire greatly.

Of course, there are bound to be overt racists in any category of people. I'm sure there are overtly racist homeschoolers, and everyone is guilty of unintentional prejudice at some time or another. The point is not that racism and prejudice don't exist, but that it is not promoted by supporting a double standard for behavior. In my experience with homeschoolers, I am encouraged to seek a high moral standard in my dealings with *all* people. Every action I take is not examined through the lens of ethnic equality, which promotes a culturally oversensitive approach to relationships. Rather, my actions are more personally judged by whether or not I am sensitive to individuals. That kind of promotion of individual sensitivity is a better approach to solving the problem of racism than allowing the double standard that exists in our schools today.

Endnotes for chapter 3:

1. Bielick, 2001; Rudner, 1999; and Ray, 1997.
2. Bielick, S., Chandler, K., and Broughman, S. P., 2001.
3. Bielick, S., and Princiotta, D., 2004.
4. The Census Bureau's Current Population Survey (CPS), and the U. S. Department of Education's National Center for Education Statistics (NCES) National Household Education Survey (NHES).
5. In fact, in 2000 the U.S. Department of Education (USDE) produced a 110-page document detailing the problems related to official counts of home educated students called *Issues relating to Estimating the Home-Schooled Population in the United States With National Household Survey Data*, NCES 2000-311, by Robin R. Henke and Phillip Kaufman.
6. U. S. Department of Education, 2000. The Census Bureau information comes from a Current Population Survey done in 1994 that was cited in the USDE document.
7. U. S. Department of Education, 1997.
8. Bielick, S., Chandler, K., and Broughman, S. P., 2001.
9. Bielick, S., and Princiotta, D., 2004.
10. Dr. Brian D. Ray is president of the National Home Education Research Institute (NHERI). The website for this non-profit organization is www.nheri.org.
11. From the Frequently Asked Questions (FAQ) page in the research section at http://www.hslda.org/research/faq.asp
12. This number came from Dr. Ray's 2002 book, <u>Worldwide Guide to Homeschooling</u>. Dr. Brian D. Ray is president of the National Home Education Research Institute (NHERI). This and other books can be obtained from the website at www.nheri.org.
13. U. S. Department of Education. National Center for Education Statistics. *The Condition of Education 2000-2005*. Retrieved June 13, 2005, from http://nces.ed.gov/programs/coe
14. Dr. Dobson has a tape called "Pulling Kids From Public School" available on the Focus on the Family website at: http://www.family.org/resources/itempg.cfm?itemid=3318 . For more information on the Southern Baptist initiative, see the Exodus Mandate website at: http://www.exodusmandate.org/

15. Gallager and Jonas, 2003.
16. Kraychir, H. R. (2003, July). *Dispelling the Stereotype of Ethnic Prejudice in Homeschooling.* Retrieved June 15, 2005, from http://homeschooling.gomilpitas.com/articles/071003.htm
17. Catalanello, 2005.
18. Ray, 1997.
19. Basham, 2001.

Concerns

"My son homeschools my grandchildren, and I don't think he's doing a good job."

I'm glad you're concerned. Sometimes concerns of that nature are warranted, and sometimes they're not. Either way, it is a good idea to really support your grandchildren and their parents in their efforts. The best way to start is to try to understand where your son is coming from. If he's doing things differently than you expected, that may be okay. Many homeschools do not look like classroom schools, and there's nothing wrong with that. They do not have to operate the same way to be effective. Teaching parents often choose different ways to educate their children, but they will still be educated in the end.

One of the most difficult forms of education for those outside the family to understand is called *unschooling*. This is where a child is educated in a way that is based upon his or her interests and needs at the time. It can look strange because the child doesn't appear to be in school. Textbooks and other school mainstays may be entirely absent, and there may be no fixed time for school.

For example, a child may show an interest in bugs, so the family will take a trip to the museum to see the entomology exhibit, get books from the library on bugs, and count and then estimate the total number of certain types of bugs they can find in their yard. They may write to science magazines asking questions about bugs that interest the child, etc. Even without textbooks the child is learning a great deal of useful information while pursuing his passion.

And, because of his interest, the skills will probably stick with the child. Because the educational process in this type of home is very closely aligned with the child's interests, other names for this method are *child-centered* or *delight-directed* learning.

Another viable approach to education that can worry concerned relatives is the *better late than early* method. This is based upon research by Dr. Raymond Moore, who was an analyst with the United States Department of Education in the 1960s. He asserted that forcing children into academics before they were ready was damaging, and readiness for academics could come much later than previously thought. In his books[1] he urged parents to consider delaying sending children to school, especially boys, until at least the age of eight. He also stated that children could wait to learn many academic tasks, like reading, until they reach that age and catch up very quickly when they were ready. They simply needed to be immersed in an academically enriching and stable environment until they were showing certain signs of readiness.

Although this may sound strange in the regimented world of grade levels, I personally know of families that have taken this approach, and it has worked for them. The children really did do well when they were ready, and really did catch up quickly and often surpass their age peers. This jump in skills usually took place between the ages of eight and eleven or so, and was very dramatic. However, this approach can be very worrisome for relatives when their eight-year-old grandchildren aren't reading well or at all yet.

Occasionally, the problem is not the home educating parent – it's the 'concerned' relative. Sometimes grandparents may feel that the decision to homeschool is a direct condemnation of their own educational decisions for their children. This may or may not be the case. Most parents make decisions simply because they believe they are in the best interests of their own children. Either way, that is more of a relationship problem than an educational one. Also, grandparents may worry that their grandchildren may not receive an adequate education if they are homeschooled. If that is the concern, then be reassured and continue reading. This book was written for you. Homeschooling has been demonstrated to be a viable form of education that produces excellent results. Children can get a first-rate education studying with their parents.

Then, of course, your son really may not be doing a very good job. Your concern may well be founded in fact. If this is the case, your tactful and non-judgmental input is vital. Try to understand your son's plan for his children. Research what you do know about his approach, and get on board. If you have a specific area of concern, express it to your son using 'I' statements such as, "I'm concerned about Melanie's progress in multiplication." It can be followed with support: "I remember a way that I learned that was really fun. Would you like me to try it with Melanie?" It is also a good idea to notice and mention the things you think your son is doing well. "Melanie is so polite that I'm sure she would be a pleasure to work with."

As a parent and a grandparent, you are in a unique position to impact your son's family in a positive way. You are a very important figure in your grandchildren's lives, and you need to be there for them in a positive way that does not belittle their parents, whom they love. As long as you don't see clear evidence of abuse (such as parental drug or alcohol abuse, significant mental illness issues, or unmistakable signs of physical abuse), though, it's important to leave the final decisions to your son and daughter-in-law.

I have known a few homeschooling parents who made what I considered to be poor educational decisions for their children. I was concerned that their children would turn out to be unprepared for life in the adult world, based on the education they received. In the overwhelming majority of cases I was wrong. Their parents simply made decisions that were different from the ones I would have made, and their children ended up doing well. In a few cases, I was right, but even then most of those children made up for lost time when they graduated and continued to learn. They have all turned out well in the end, even though I was concerned in the middle. Hopefully, that will be the case for your son as well.

"My friend is a teacher, and she says a child who had been homeschooled was enrolled in her class, and he's not up to grade level."

Some kids do not operate 'at grade level.' Grade level is an artificial measurement based upon an average and often geared toward school curricula. Even though home education has a good record for producing above average students, not every one will achieve that standard. In order for above average students to exist, there must be average and below average students to balance out that score.

Another thing to consider is that sometimes children who enter school after homeschooling, especially in the elementary school years, are sent to school because home education wasn't working for them. In other words, these are the children whose parents didn't feel that they were doing as good a job as the school could do, so they sent their children to school. They were being responsible to give their children what they thought was the better option for them, and in that case, they thought school would be better for them than homeschooling. Rather than criticizing them, we should be supporting these parents and encouraging them to continue to be involved.

It is important to note that there are a significant number of children who struggle in school, too. According to the United States Department of Education in 2003, 37 percent of fourth graders and 26 percent of eighth graders performed at the "below basic" level in reading. 23 percent of fourth graders and 32 percent of eighth graders were "below basic" in mathematics. In 2002, 26 percent of 12th graders were "below basic" in reading, and only 5 percent tested at the "advanced" reading level needed to succeed in college.[2] That is why there are so many initiatives to require children to pass tests to graduate from school; one-fourth of our children did not graduate able to read at the level necessary to function in society.

Some state laws have clauses in them that require home educated children who do not operate at grade level to be forced to enter school. So what should be done with the schoolchildren who are academically "below basic?" Should they be required to learn at home? Homeschools have a much better record for turning out educated adults who are happy and involved in their communities than most schools, as research can confirm.

"I know some homeschoolers, and they're weird."

Well, I know several weird kids who attend school, too. The truth is that weird parents tend to have weird children. Some homeschoolers are weird, just as some public schoolers and some private schoolers are. Home education didn't make them weird – they started out that way. And, chances·are the weird parents who are raising the weird children you mention were educated in public or private schools. Did their form of education make them weird?

Who gets to say what's weird, anyway? Some weirdness is not necessarily a bad thing. I am grateful that our constitution allowed for the weirdness that produced some of the greatest minds in American history — including Benjamin Franklin, Abraham Lincoln, and Thomas Edison — who were all considered weird by their communities as children. In their cases, the problem was not based in the 'weird' children themselves, but in the communities that would not accept their differences.

That is a common source of the label of weirdness — an unwillingness to think outside the box and acknowledge the uniqueness of an individual as a positive thing. There are some people whose strange approaches to things are not positive or negative, but just different. Since that is not a criminal thing, it is probably okay to accept them just the way they are. Also, some people think homeschooling is inherently weird, so in their minds all homeschoolers are weird. Although I'm not saying that your acquaintances are not strange, I am saying that you might consider the possibility that their weirdness might be a positive thing. Or, then again, they might just be weird, and that's okay.

"How do we know the children aren't being abused? Does homeschooling contribute to child abuse?"

How do 'we' know any child is not being abused? As a special education teacher, I worked in community and private programs with chemically-dependent and disturbed children and teenagers. Many of them had been abused. Although some were reported by school officials, the majority had parents, relatives, or police officers bring them in for help. Daily scrutiny in school was not sufficient to detect or protect many of them from abuse. Child abuse has always occurred, and those who do it have always been very creative about ways to circumvent the law. In those cases, the problem is not the law – it is those disturbed individuals who choose to abuse their children.

Some people are afraid that home education may happen in such isolation that abuse can be easily hidden. I don't think that is the case. Home educators, as I pointed out before, are rarely stereotypically isolated hermits who never see anyone else. They come into contact with neighbors (often suspicious neighbors, I might add), doctors (who are mandatory reporters), and a variety of other people, including other home educators, in daily life. Even when people try to 'prove' how easy it is to hide, they have a hard time. In October of 2003 CBS ran a special that hinted that homeschoolers could hide abuse.[3] They discussed a few tragic cases where supposedly home-schooled children had been abused (many were not in compliance with homeschool laws). However, ALL the families they highlighted had been involved with protective services. None were hidden. I don't believe it is nearly as easy to hide as some fear it is.

I am more concerned about the average school than the average home. Here are some school crime statistics from the 2003 School Crime and Safety Report[4]:

- "Between 7 and 9 percent of students in grades 9-12 reported being threatened or injured with a weapon such as a gun, knife or club on school property in the preceding 12 months" in every report from 1993 to 2001. (p. viii)
- "In 2001, 8 percent of 12- through 18-year-old students reported being bullied at school in the last 6 months, up from 5 percent in 1999." (p. viii) The report alludes to the fact that bullying tends to be more common than this with younger children, and mentions a 14 percent rate for sixth-graders. (p.16)
- "In 1999-2000, *20 percent* [emphasis mine – that's one out of five!] of all public schools experienced one or more serious violent crimes such as rape, sexual assault, robbery, and aggravated assault. Seventy-one percent of schools reported at least one violent incident." (Executive summary, p viii) "…secondary schools were more likely to have a violent incident than elementary, middle, and combined schools (92 percent vs. 61-87 percent for the other school levels)." [Note: "…violent incidents include rape, sexual battery other than rape, physical attack or fight with or without a weapon, threat of physical attack with or without a weapon,

and robbery with or without a weapon." *Serious* violent incidents are a subset of violent incidents.] (p. 20)

- Teachers aren't safe in schools, either. "...from 1997 to 2001, teachers were the victims of 473,000 violent crimes (rape or sexual assault, robbery, aggravated assault, and simple assault)." About 48,000 of those were considered *serious* violent crimes. (p. 28)

- Students feel unsafe at school, too. "In both 1999 and 2001, students were more likely to be afraid of being attacked when they were at school than away from school." (p.ix) That makes sense, because "between 1993 and 2001 the percentage of students in grades 9-12 who reported carrying a weapon such as a gun, knife, or club on school property within the previous thirty days declined from 12 percent to 6 percent." (p. ix) Although the report states this reduced percentage with optimism, we should still be shocked. Six percent? Out of every 50 students, three of them are carrying some kind of self-described weapon? Yikes!

Compare those statistics to 2002 numbers on child abuse[5]: "906,000 children in the United States were confirmed by child protective service agencies as being maltreated." Of those, "61% experienced neglect; 19% were physically abused; 10% were sexually abused; and 5% were emotionally or psychologically abused." This translates to 1.8 percent of the approximately 50 million school-aged children in the United States. Assuming that only one-fourth of the actual cases gets reported, as many as 5 percent of the population of children in the United States may be abused or neglected, with almost 2 percent of those abused.

That projection is still lower than the actual number of children who report being bullied (8 percent), or threatened or injured with a weapon on school property (7-9 percent). So, although abuse can happen, the incidence of regular, documented abuse in schools is still higher than estimates of possible child abuse of all types in the total population. Based on these statistics, I'd have to say that schools are more dangerous places for children than homes.

I believe that there are many things that contribute to child abuse, including but not limited to: human depravity, a culture where children and the weak are not valued, high-stress lives, constant exposure and desensitization to violence and anti-social behavior in the media and at school, the lack of positive bonding in families, divorce (especially serial parental relationships) and the stress of single parenting, mental health problems, and drug and alcohol abuse. I do not, however, believe that home education contributes to child abuse. Based upon reporting requirements, abuse statistics, and my personal experience with home educators, I believe the incidence of abuse is much lower among homeschoolers than among publicly and privately schooled children.

Home education may actually reduce some of the contributing factors. Most parents who choose to educate their children at home value them highly and set a high priority on relationships. Home educated children tend to come from two-parent families, so stress factors associated with single parenting are reduced. The likelihood that the parent may be unaware of abuse by other family members or strangers is also reduced, since parents who spend a lot of time with their children get pretty tuned in to them. So, although there is the risk of child abuse any time a child is born, home education does not contribute to that risk. It may even reduce the risk.

Endnotes for chapter 4:

1. Better Late Than Early and School Can Wait are two well-known examples of Dr. Moore's work.
2. U. S. Department of Education. National Center for Education Statistics. *The Condition of Education 2000-2005*. Retrieved June 13, 2005, from http://nces.ed.gov/help/sitemap.asp
3. This two-part series ran October 14th and 15th, 2003. Transcripts retrieved on the Internet at http://www.cbsnews.com/stories/2003/10/13/eveningnews/main577817.shtml
4. From the "Indicators of School Crime and Safety: 2003" report put out by joint efforts of the National Center for Education Statistics (NCES) and the Bureau of Justice Statistics (BJS). The numbers cited here were mostly from the executive summary at the beginning of the report.
5. According to the National Center for Injury Prevention and Control, a division of the Centers for Disease Control and Prevention.

Personal Sacrifices

"What about your own lives as parents? As husband and wife?"

This is something to think about. You should not homeschool without considering how it will affect you, your life, and your marriage. In some cases you may decide that it's not worth it to change your life to home educate your children. If that's the way you feel you need to acknowledge it and act accordingly. If you choose to teach your children at home, you have to spend time with them and take the responsibility of supervising them. This can interfere with your ability to participate in many activities that do not include children. It is also important to assess your willingness to be habitually on duty. You might just say that that's the price of being a parent, no matter how or where you choose to educate your children.

Children are an incredible blessing, but many parents are not prepared for the rigors of child-rearing. Sadly, many of us were raised in the 'me' generation, and our focus remains on ourselves. This is not an impossible hurdle to overcome for the motivated parent, however. Support is available for those of us who need a little extra help learning how to raise our children in a positive way without burning ourselves out.

You don't have to give up all outside adult interests, either. I still attend women's groups from church and do other things I like to do without children. It is important to set priorities to determine which activities are really necessary and which are not, though. You really can't do everything. There are many fun things you can do *with* your children, too, that are not necessarily child-centered. Our family does lots of things together with our children that we all enjoy, like volunteering to feed people in our community, for example.

As parents we should remember that children keep on growing, and we won't ever have this time with them again. If we don't find ways to be with them and enjoy them now, we will miss out on some pretty extraordinary moments. I firmly believe that each child is special, placed in each family for an important purpose. If we focus on ourselves too much during their formative years, we will have lost an opportunity that we will never be able to retrieve. There will be time to pursue other interests later.

Although it is vitally important to make time with your spouse alone, homeschooling can bring you closer as well. My husband and I feel we are working toward a common goal. Since we are working together in the home education process – a very important thing to do – we spend time talking about our hopes and dreams not just for our children, but for ourselves as well. Also, teaching our children ourselves has made us think outside the box and make things happen that we want to have happen. This attitude can spill over into other aspects of our lives, and we have done many things I never would have considered possible otherwise. In all, homeschooling has helped to make me more satisfied with some aspects of my life.

"How do you keep the house clean?"

I have a confession to make — I don't. I try to get it clean on a regular basis, but am not as successful as I want to be. On any given day, there will be toys scattered in the yard, and a variety of personal items and projects in various stages throughout in the house. However, I just take that as evidence that I have a house full of happy, active children. I can't do everything, and that's okay. I am working at a full-time job. Imagine trying to work in a school environment where you are not only the teacher, but also the janitor, cafeteria worker, bus driver, etc. It's pretty hard to be an expert at everything.

However, that doesn't mean you have to live in a pigsty. This is a great time to give children responsibilities, and help them to understand their part in the family system. If they were at school all day and returned home to find the house clean, they would never realize how much work it took to get it that way. Or, if they only came home to sleep, they might not realize just how dirty a lived-in house can get if you don't work at keeping it clean. When they are a part of the process, they get the chance to see and participate in the work of the household. This is an important life skill.

Although I wish I were a better housekeeper, I am pleased that my children know they are needed and are learning their parts in getting and keeping the house in order. Your spouse can be a great help in this endeavor, too. Remember – homeschooling is a full-time job. If you worked outside of the home, s/he would be able to see the need for help. Being at home does not make it easier to keep the house clean; it just means the house has more people using it all the time. My better organized friends do a good job of having their houses quite clean when I am visiting, so I know it is possible. Many of them even manage to keep it clean when they don't have guests! Amazing! It simply takes some thought and problem-solving.

If you are a fastidious housekeeper, teaching your children at home may make you rethink your priorities – or at least enlist the help of your spouse and kids to keep the house in good order. I suggest, however, that the children are a higher priority than the house. For those of you who struggle even when the kids are in school, you might want to work out a plan for keeping the house clean before you start homeschooling. Who knows? With a little extra thought applied to the process, things might get better when everyone gets involved.

"Wouldn't it be easier just to go to work and send them to school?"

The quick answer to that question is, yes, it probably would be easier in most circumstances, but that wasn't our experience. Homeschooling is the most comprehensive job I have ever held, and I've held some doozies. However, that doesn't mean it isn't worth it. When I sent my two oldest girls to school in first and second grade, I soon discovered that it wasn't as much easier as I thought it would be. They came home from school stressed about the social situations they found themselves in, and there was little time to spend with them. So, I gave up some happy children to the school system, and it sent back stressed children with bad social habits (gossip, clique-ishness, lying, and others).

I didn't have enough time with them to fully deal with some of the problems they experienced. I helped each one of them with homework, got their clothes ready for the next day, and made lunches, but I lost many of the fun parts of raising my children. I didn't get to see them reach some major developmental milestones. I missed the "opportunity moments" I had always shared with my children, where they asked me deep questions triggered by some incident of daily life, and we would just spend time talking about those important things. They didn't remember their questions by the time they got home, and they couldn't ask the teacher during classes, so they were just learning not to ask.

Simply getting them out the door in the morning with home-work, signed forms, and lunch money was a monumental task. When my daughters had trouble with homework, I had to figure out what they had been taught and what they hadn't. I had one daughter who was taking more time doing homework each day than she had spent doing all of her formal school work the year before, and this was after a full day of school! It wasn't even an efficient use of her time, since she rarely understood her homework until I taught her what she needed to know before she could get started.

Of course, I didn't earn any extra money by sending my children to school, and I know that is a factor for many people. That leads to the next question...

"How can you afford to live on one income?"

In our society we get really used to things that are truly nonessential. It boils down to priorities. My children are high priori-ties, so we make do. Sure, it probably would be easier for our family financially if I took a full-time job. However, I know that my children don't do as well in school as they do learning at home. They are thriving now, so I put aside my desire to get a new couch for the living room and do what I can to fill in the cracks in household income. I tutor to pay for the tutorial my older daughters are involved in, and look for ways to earn extra money while staying at home with the kids (how are you enjoying this book?). It can be done. It just takes a little determination and resolve. This is the decision I've made, and I'm glad I did. The fruit I'm seeing in my children is worth more than a completely remodeled house. While a new couch would be nice, the character of my children will outlast the best of new couches. I'd rather put my time and attention into what lasts, rather than in what is temporary. One of my favorite quotes is from Jim Elliot, a martyred missionary to South America: "He is no fool who gives up what he cannot keep to gain what he cannot lose."

Sending children to school while you work is often not as cheap as you think it is. Obviously, if you send them to a private school, tuition is a big factor. But even if you send them to public schools, there are many expenses. When we added up the costs involved in sending classroom supplies, personal supplies, mandatory fund-raisers, PTA membership, lunch boxes, nicer school clothes, and other little 'extras' that we did not need while teaching them at home, we found that our expenses were similar to the previous year. It really adds up, even if your children are not in after-school activities.

Then there is before and after school care for many families, which is a huge expense. Now think about some of the extra costs that come with working: taxes, lunch away from home, clothes that fit the work environment, gas, prepared meals and fast food, and the fund-raisers held in the office. There are actually many more, but they seem so small that they're easy to overlook.

It's actually pretty expensive to work, and the amount of your salary that goes to paying these expenses for school and work is mind-boggling. Estimates have been put forth in past years by a number of 'experts' about how much second income it requires for a married mother of two just to break even. They ranged across tens of thousands of dollars, depending upon earning potential. This is NOT what is required to buy new curtains or couches, or even shoes. This is what it takes to break even – just to cover the expenses of working outside the home! Consider how much you are really contributing to the family income if you subtract all the expenses associated with working and sending your kids to school.[1]

Is it really worth it? If your answer is a resounding yes, then you have made a fine decision for yourself and your family. However, if you are wondering if it really *is* worth it, then you understand my position and the decision many home educators have made in this regard. It's not actually as big a sacrifice as some people think it is.

"Don't you want to get out sometimes?"

Sure! So, I do! I am not shackled to the house and the children. Now, don't get me wrong – I DO spend a lot of time with my children, and a lot of time at home. And yes, there are times when I just want to call up some neighbor and send my kids over there for a while. However, even bad days end eventually, and then I am glad I do what I do. I really am free to make my own schedule. Often I do end up cooking supper and spending the evening with my family at home, but there are a few exceptions: Mondays, when my kids spend some time at a friends or they come to my house and my son has football practice, Tuesdays, when I tutor, Wednesdays, when we are at church, Thursdays, when we go to our homeschool tutorial and have football practice, Saturdays, when we have football games or family excursions, and Sundays, when we go to church and volunteer in the community. I guess the bigger problem would be trimming our schedule to have a little more time at home! There's a joke that runs through home education circles about "carschooling," and everyone always understands it.

In fact, that's a common problem homeschool families often face – remembering to say "no" to things that sound fun but take up more time than they really have. When your time is self-directed, it is tempting to think of it as free time when it is not. *Flexible time is not the same as free time.* Family time needs to be written into the calendar if you value it. Some people want more home time, while others want more out time. It's a personality thing. If everyone remembers that their calendar is their own, then that can come into balance. That's another benefit of home education — when you take control of your children's schedules, you begin to realize that you have more control than you thought over your own as well. If you want to get out more often and can balance everyone's needs, then just do it. If you want to stay home more often, then make it a priority.

That attitude has been the most freeing aspect of staying home for me — the understanding that no one else is controlling the way I live my life. In contrast to the way I felt when I was trying to work my schedule around the school year, homework, and school activities, I now know that I am in control of my life and my time. I have to get certain things done, but how and when I do that is up to me. Keeping a homeschool schedule has helped me realize that I am not only responsible for what goes on in my life and in the lives of my children; I don't have to do things the way everyone else does them. If I don't like my situation, I can change it.

"I'm afraid being a stay-at-home mom would keep me from a fulfilling life."

As you look for ways to stimulate your child in his or her areas of interest, you may discover dormant interests of your own that you didn't have time to discover or develop before. Apples don't fall far from the tree, after all. When you don't have to follow someone else's plan for your time every day, you can take the time to explore your own areas of interest.

That's not even taking into account the attraction parents have for their children. Kids are pretty interesting and stimulating just by themselves. Have you ever taken the time to watch children in a new situation? The wonder they show is contagious. It really is true that your children keep you young.

Before World War II, bright women often stayed at home and raised children, and no one accused them of throwing away their lives. That's because society realized that they were fulfilling an essential purpose in their world – preparing the next generation for its part in the culture. Literacy rates were higher then, and crime rates were lower. It wasn't until after World War II that families realized that not only could they have a lot more *stuff* if women worked outside the home, but working was also *easier* than staying at home and raising kids. The American dream changed from being able to *do* more to being able to *have* more. In addition, because of the postwar boom, the increase in labor-saving devices, and the modernized school systems, women felt that they were not contributing as much at home as they could in the work force. So, many began to work outside the home as soon as their children were school-aged.

The effects of that era became evident by the time of the rebellious Sixties and the sexual revolution of the Seventies. When men left their homes to work in factories at the time of the industrial revolution, children's behavior started to deteriorate. Once women also left their homes to work, it reached a crisis point. As those children grew up, crime increased to levels heretofore unknown in western society. Selfish behaviors were at record levels as parents replaced *time with* their children with *stuff for* their children. Children never practiced the healthy interdependence that is so essential to contributing positively to society.

The results confirmed what we should have known all along. CHILDREN NEED PARENTS. They need parents who are not stressed out and overworked, and who know what is going on with them. When the children in a society are secure, the future of that society is secure. When parents are doing what they are called to do, and are taking the time to really know their children, their children are secure. Thus, those who help make secure children are providing for the future of their society. What could be more fulfilling than that?

"How do you handle being with the kids all the time?"

Some people don't like spending time with their children. That's a sad fact in our culture. It's difficult to spend time with people when you don't know what to do with them, especially if you are supposed to be "in charge." I think that's an under-recognized crisis in our nation. Parents are increasingly bombarded with confusing messages about issues such as discipline and child development, and are unfamiliar with the parenting skills that make raising a family more fun.

I understand. You know how some people are natural moms? They're the ones who carried dolls all through their childhoods and dreamed of what it would be like to be married and have children someday. Well, I'm not one of those. I dreamed of being president, or going to the moon, or discovering a new kind of fossil on an uninhabited island somewhere. Somehow I never really thought about being a mom. Oh, I *wanted* children, and I imagined *having* children, but I never really thought about the process of raising them.

Learning to parent has not been easy, but the investment I have put into my children has paid off more than I ever could have imagined at the beginning of this journey. They are giving *me* so much more than I ever thought possible. One of the best benefits of my efforts is the discovery that I'm raising kids I like. They're cute, funny, and interesting. I like being with them.

I'm not with them *all* the time, though. Teaching my kids does not mean that they spend every minute of every day with me. They are in church groups, classes, music lessons, ball games, etc., when I am not directly in charge of them. They also spend the night with friends, go to camp in the summer, and attend Vacation Bible School. During the days they have time to play with each other and to spend alone, which is a luxury few children seem to have these days. It's not unusual for my crew of four to go off and build a pioneer village in the woods, or make a Moon station, or play basketball in the back yard. They also choose to spend a lot of their time reading. That makes for a lot of peaceful time for me.

I do spend more time with my kids than some other moms, however, and I'm glad. When they were in school I didn't get enough time to see how they were really doing in the short time between homework, supper, and baths. I didn't get the time to influence their personalities or truly know them at the level I do now. I spent a lot less undirected time with them just finding out what was important to them and sharing my own heart with them. It's easy to enjoy someone you spend a lot of time with and know well.

Maybe that's the key – some parents don't enjoy spending much time with their children because they don't really know them well – and maybe their children (especially teens) aren't thrilled to spend time with their parents for the same reason. They don't know what to do together. They haven't worked at developing *common* interests. In any committed, intimate relationship, you take risks and spend time doing things with the other person. You take the good with the bad, sharing joys and forgiving freely. That's just part of discovering the depths of the other person's being.

The good news about this is that this process can start at any time. Parents *can* learn how to enjoy spending time with their children. All of our nation's children, homeschooled or not, can experience the wonderful ups and downs of growing truly intimate with parents they can trust. They can learn how to get close and stay intimate, and thus avoid some of the pitfalls of superficial relationships so prevalent in our society. It just takes a conscious effort.

"It may be fine for you, but homeschooling would be too hard for me."

Any time you try to do something you don't want to do, it will be hard. If you don't feel it is what you want to do or it is not right for your family, don't do it. Homeschooling is not for everyone. However, don't let fear keep you from homeschooling if it is what you really want to do. Homeschooling is not as hard as it may seem, and public school is not as easy as it seems. For me, educating my children at home is easier than sending them to school. We have more time to play together and get other things done than before, and they are less stressed out.

Also, I am raising kids that I like (most of the time!). That takes a lot of the stress out of the job. There is no question that it can be difficult to be 'on duty' with the kids most of the time, especially if you are also trying to keep the house clean, cook, keep up with friends and your spouse, etc. However, if that is addressed, some job-sharing and a weekly outing can alleviate much of that stress. If you understand that this is only a season of your life, and it will pass more quickly than you think, that helps with the hard days when some look-alike, badly-behaved aliens swapped places with your kids for a while.

Some people are afraid of the academic responsibilities, and that is a valid concern. However, with all the resources available to home educators these days, that part is getting easier and easier. Most homeschooling parents get support from other home educators in the form of support groups, co-ops or tutorials, on-line message boards or chat rooms, or from friends and neighbors with expertise in a given subject area. That way, "Parent A" can get help from "Parent B" in teaching writing, while offering help in math or science, for example.

Those kinds of resources also help when there are personal problems with a particular child or situation, even if it seems unrelated to education. Most homeschoolers see education as part of a lifestyle, so relationship issues are common topics for discussion.

Homeschool tutorials and cooperatives are springing up all

over, too, where home educators pool their resources to create classes. In a cooperative, parents take turns teaching classes in their areas of expertise. In a tutorial, parents hire tutors to teach more difficult classes to groups of students. So, while home education often looks daunting to the outsider, it is much more "do-able" than many parents imagine.

Some parents who think homeschooling would be too hard are imagining teaching their children in the way they were taught — with the structure and materials used in schools. Well, that would be too hard for me, too. One of the greatest benefits of educating your children yourself is that you don't have to imitate group schooling. It's flexible, and the only thing that really matters is the outcome. Learning can be natural and integrated into everything you do, rather than forced in an unnatural setting. A science unit can start with a video, progress to checking out some materials from the library, and end with a letter to a scientific association or a speech in front of the local 4-H club. Or, if you and your child enjoy or need the structure of textbooks, you can use them flexibly in a way that meets your needs. You can spend more or less time on a subject if needed to make sure you really understand it.

When you have the freedom to learn things along with your children, the pressure to be a know-it-all teacher fades. When your children become self-motivated learners, the pressure to learn everything your children learn also diminishes. So, home education becomes the method of a more relaxed, enjoyable lifestyle of learning than a difficult task set before you. I don't want to give the impression that homeschooling is easy, however. It takes dedication and purpose to do anything worth doing, and teaching your own children is no exception. It is not the realm of the lazy. It just is not the exclusive territory of the superhuman workhorse, either.

"I would homeschool, if I got along with my child."

It is amazing to me how often I hear this type of comment. First of all, I had no idea that so many people were considering homeschooling. Secondly, why would relationship problems with a child keep a parent from doing something that often improves relationships in the family? I guess what they're really saying is, "I just don't want to be confined with a difficult child and put in the work it takes to understand that child." I think they're hoping the problems will go away with time.

If there is a relationship problem in your family, it will not just go away. It needs to be dealt with. No matter where or when the problem is occurring, the parent needs to take the lead in confronting the problem and eliminating it, if possible. You don't have to homeschool to do this, but educating children at home does offer parents and children more time to work on their relationships with each other in a natural way. This happens without conscious effort when your life's focus is on each other. If you have them with you most of the time, you MUST deal with problems as they come up; you simply can't ignore what is right in front of you. You may choose to get help with the problem, and this is often wise, but there is a definite motivation to see to it that the problem is not just *out of your face*, but that it is *solved*.

For the people who think homeschooling is only for perfect parents, or for those with great relationships with their kids, I have one thing to say – *no one is perfect*. Homeschoolers are no less human than the rest of the world. Most of us struggle to find the right balance between discipline and nurture, friendship and authority. As a dedicated parent, I refuse to give up until I find that balance. Although it is not usually listed as a positive part of home education, I think it is one of the most essential positives – the necessity of dealing with relationship and personal problems as they come up. This prevents many longer term, more serious problems from developing.

Endnotes for chapter 5:
1. The Moms at Home Success webpage has a cost of work calculator that might interest you. Just click on the link in the second paragraph at http://www.momsathomesuccess.com

The History of Homeschooling, the Law, and Research

"When did homeschooling begin?"

Actually, a better question would be, "When did compulsory education begin?" Before the 1850's in the United States, and throughout most of human history, home education was the rule. In fact, when compulsory schooling was first introduced in Massachusetts, parents refused to comply. The military had to be deployed to force parents to give up their children, dragged kicking and screaming from their homes to school. Sheldon Richman describes this in his book, <u>Separating School & State: How To Liberate American Families</u>: "In 1852, [Massachusetts] set up the first modern government schooling system. It was not always smooth going for the enforcers, however. Some 80 percent of the people of Massachusetts resisted the imposition of public schooling. In 1880, it took the militia to persuade the parents of Barnstable, on Cape Cod, to give up their children to the system."[1]

Part of the problem probably had to do with the philosophical roots of compulsory schooling. Our school system is primarily based on the Prussian system, which was the first modern nation to embark on the compulsory schooling journey. After being defeated by Napoleon in 1806, Prussia's elite decided that their country needed masses of soldiers and workers that would obey quickly and without thinking, like Napoleon's army did. The schools that formed as a result of that determination laid the foundation for many school programs worldwide, including those in the United States. John Taylor Gatto wrote in his essay, *The Public School Nightmare*, "So the world got compulsion schooling at the end of a state bayonet for the first time in human history; modern forced schooling started in Prussia in 1819 with a clear vision of what centralized schools could deliver: 1. Obedient soldiers to the army; 2. Obedient workers to the mines; 3. Well subordinated civil servants to government; 4. Well subordinated clerks to industry; and 5. Citizens who thought alike about major issues." He went on later to say, "You need to know this because over the first 50 years of our school institution[,] Prussian purpose—which was to create a form of state socialism—gradually forced out traditional American purpose, which in most minds was to prepare the individual to be self-reliant."[2]

"Mandatory kindergarten was necessary for the masses because it served to break the influence of the mother over the child thus making the child more responsive to government influence."[3] Individualization was discouraged and academics were presented in such a way that sustained thinking would become difficult. Knowledge would be broken into subjects, subtopics, and thinking would be halted regularly by horns telling them to change the focus of their thoughts. Memorization and regimentation were the keys to this new way of schooling children. The theory was that workers taught this way would fulfill their places in society, be easily controlled and happy in dull roles in society, and that they would not think dangerous, anti-social and revolutionary thoughts. They would, however, make a good army.

These schools were observed and praised by several wealthy Americans in the early 1800's. Many politicians had hopes that compulsory schools, or 'common' schools, as they were called, would keep the 'lower' classes more child-like and more dependent upon group mentality, and that would mostly eliminate crime in this country. Horace Mann, an early proponent of compulsory Prussian schools in the United States, wrote in his *Common School Journal* in 1841, "Let the Common School be expanded to its capabilities, let it be worked with the efficiency of which it is susceptible, and nine tenths of the crimes in the penal code would become obsolete; the long catalogue of human ills would be abridged; men would walk more safely by day; every pillow would be more inviolate by night; property, life, and character held by a stronger tenure; all rational hopes respecting the future brightened."[4]

Many well-positioned men went to Prussia to earn this country's first Ph.D.'s, including Edward Everett, the future Governor of Massachusetts, and Horace Mann, who served as a leader in the Massachusetts legislature and helped establish the Massachusetts Board of Education. It is no accident that Massachusetts was the first to push compulsory schooling through its legislature.

Unfortunately, compulsory schooling did not abolish prisons or make our streets safer. It did, however, get expanded to its capabilities. The result was disastrous for our nation. Diane Alden describes this when she writes, "In the year 1941 the Defense Department was preparing for World War II. In testing 18 million men between 1941 and 1944, the Defense Department found 96 percent of those tested were literate. During this same period, among African Americans who were tested—the majority of whom had only three years of schooling—80 percent were found to be literate. By literate we mean that Americans, both white and black, could read with understanding.

During the Korean War the Department of Defense tested three million men for service and only 19 percent were found to be literate. In less then 10 years there had been a 500 percent rise in illiteracy. Perplexed, the Defense Department investigated and found that the same test had been used during the two wars and the only difference was that those men and women tested during the Korean War had more schooling—at a significantly higher cost".[5]

For a more thorough treatment of the history of American Education, consider reading the works of John Taylor Gatto or Sheldon Richman, or doing an Internet search using the phrase 'Prussian Schools.' Clearly, compulsory schooling did not arise from a desire to make sure that all children had a chance to reach their full potential. Perhaps that is why the highly literate parents in Massachusetts objected to this experiment being performed on their children.

Adults in the United States today have a hard time imagining anything *but* compulsory schooling. Although there have always been 'underground' home educators, home education did not reemerge as a visible movement until the 1960's, about 100 years after the first compulsory schooling laws.

Some of the first visible homeschoolers were radical parents who followed the advice of former New York teacher-of-the-year John Holt in his book *How Children Fail*.[6] Mr. Holt asserted that traditional schools dehumanized children and stripped them of original thought. People who followed Mr. Holt's ideals tended to teach their children in a more natural, less schoolish way that resonated with the culture of the sixties. His organization called Growing Without Schooling (GWS) influenced many parents, and this is still a popular way to educate children.

Another influence on home education in the 1960's and 1970's was United States Department of Education analyst Dr. Raymond Moore. In his books, including Better Late than Early,[7] he asserted that it is damaging to force children into school at an early age, and that it would be better to keep children in a home environment until much later. Formal schooling should begin no earlier than the age of eight or so. As a former missionary, Dr. Moore appealed more to conservative Christian parents. The *better late than early* approach is also still very popular.

Although I have listed two prominent influences, there were actually many more people who were public advocates of home education in those days and in the years that followed. Some names that might come up as influential people in the modern homeschooling movement, in no particular order, include: John Holt and his successor at GWS, Patrick Farenga, Raymond Moore, Phyllis Schlafly (a pro-family leader), John Taylor Gatto (another teacher of the year who despises schools), J. Michael Smith and Michael P. Farris (president, and former president and founder of the Home School Legal Defense Association), and many, many more...

"Are there any famous homeschoolers in history?"

The easy answer to that question is yes. I have gathered a small list of famous people who were partially or completely homeschooled. All would be considered home educated if they were taught in similar ways today, although I have included some people who were mostly self-educated, because their self-education had a drive similar to that of some home educated students today. Most had access to other forms of education, but tutors, governesses and parental home education were the rule until the late 1800s among educated families, depending on their personal resources. Elite educations in the past generally consisted of private tutors at home, often supervised and supplemented by educated parents so those children would not *have to* attend school.

I have tried to include a variety of admirable people whose educational backgrounds were unconventional, to show that there was no one road to success for them, and that what has become 'traditional' schooling was not necessary for their success. As I edited and researched the lists I started with, I was reminded of a fact that should be brought to light – for most of our history in the U.S. it was expected that children would attend school only after they were taught to read, write, and do basic arithmetic by their parents. So, by modern definitions, most well-educated historical figures started out learning at home. It is also interesting to note that few historical accounts include any mention of a school experience before university-level training.

I have omitted many names simply because their experiences were similar to others on this list or others of their generation, including most of our early presidents and 'founding fathers', who were mostly prepared for University at home by parents and/or tutors. I have also omitted most of those self-educated people who appear to have had no access to education due to poverty or lack of opportunity. Many, many famous people born before 1945 or so attended school sporadically in their early years, so I have also omitted many of their names.

Obviously, then, this is not a comprehensive or infallible list and represents a very sketchy internet search. For whatever it's worth, though, here it is:

Abigail Adams — First Lady; wife of 2nd President John Adams and mother of 6th President John Quincy Adams (b. 1744; self-educated through avid reading)

John Quincy Adams — 6th U.S. President (b. 1767; educated at home as other children were at the time. I included his name because of the detailed description given at: http://www.forerunner.com/mandate/X0069_The_Education_of_Joh.html)

Ansel Adams — Photographer known for black and white images (b. 1902; removed from school in 1915 because he hated it and was tutored at home from that point on)

Clara Barton — Red Cross Founder (b. 1821; entirely educated at home)

Alexander Graham Bell — Inventor best known for inventing the telephone (b. 1847; attended some school from ages 10-14)

Pearl S. Buck — Writer known for <u>The Good Earth</u> and other stories (b. 1892; taught in China primarily by her missionary mother and a Chinese tutor)

George Rogers Clark — American Colonel during the Revolutionary War (b. 1739; home educated by an uncle)

Henry Clay — Fiery orator and legislator in the early 1800's (b. 1777; formal schooling was limited to three years)

Agatha Christie — Writer best known for her mysteries (b. 1890; educated by her mother at home until the age of 16)

Francis S. Collins — Director of the National Human Genome Research Institute (b. late 1940's; homeschooled until the sixth grade; see http://www.genome.gov/10001018 for more information)

Pierre Curie — Scientist known for research into radiation along with his wife, Marie Curie (b. 1859; had "unconventional" education at home prior to entering the Sorbonne)

Thomas Edison — Prolific inventor known as "The Wizard of Menlo Park" (b. 1847; spent 3 months in school — intentionally removed and homeschooled by mother)

Jonathan Edwards — Evangelist associated with Christian revival in the 1740's and 1750's (b. 1703; "rigorously" homeschooled by father before entering Yale at almost 13 years of age)

Benjamin Franklin — Well-known statesman, printer and inventor known as a founding father in this country (b. 1706; approximately 2 years in school, from age 8 to 10)

Hanson — Musical group consisting of three brothers (b. 1980, 1983, 1985; see http://www.hanson.net/ for more information)

Patrick Henry — Revolutionary War statesman (b. 1736; mostly homeschooled by his father and uncle)

Robert E. Lee — Confederate General and gifted leader (b. 1807; mostly taught by his mother)

C.S. Lewis — Christian writer known for the Chronicles of Narnia and other Christian books (b. 1898; educated by his mother until her death in 1908)

Abraham Lincoln — 16th U.S. President known for The Emancipation Proclamation (b. 1809; He only went to school for about a year, in bits and pieces, and was mostly self-educated)

Douglas MacArthur – U.S. General during World War II and the Korean War (b. 1880; not much formal elementary schooling)

John Marshall — Chief Justice of the United States in the early 1800's (b. 1755; first tutor at the age of 12 after being taught to read and being given access to a good library nearby; formal education very sporadic and limited)

Yehudi Menuhin — Violinist who was famous by age 7 (b. 1916; homeschooled by choice by his mother)

John Stuart Mill — Brilliant economist (b. 1806; deliberately and systematically homeschooled by his father; see http://www.utilitarianism.com/millauto/index.html for his autobiography)

Moffats — Canadian musical group of four teen brothers, including a group of triplets (b. 1983 and 1984; 4 boys homeschooled while performing)

Sir Patrick Moore — Astronomer best known for presenting *The Sky at Night* television shows (b. 1923; educated at home because of illness)

Wolfgang Amadeus Mozart — Brilliant Austrian composer and child prodigy (b. 1756; probably tutored exclusively by his father, who we know tutored his sister)

Frankie Muniz — Actor known as the star of the *Agent Cody Banks* films (b. 1985)

Sean O'Casey — Irish idealist and writer (b. 1880; no formal schooling because of an eye disease)

George Patton — U.S. General best known for his abrasive manner and daring assaults during World War II (b. 1885; first formal schooling at age 11)

Christopher Paolini — Best-selling science fiction author (b. 1984; entirely homeschooled and graduated high school at 15)

LeAnn Rimes — Singer known for prodigious talents at an early age (b. 1982; homeschooled to allow for her music career; see http://www.leannrimes.com/ for more information)

Franklin Delano Roosevelt — 32nd U.S. President known for the New Deal and his leadership through the Great Depression and World War II (b. 1882; mother supervised education by tutors until the age of 14)

Theodore Roosevelt — 26th U.S. President known to "Speak softly and carry a big stick" (b. 1901; entirely educated by tutors because of sickness)

Andrei Sakharov — 1975 Nobel Peace Prize winner in nuclear physics (b. 1921; homeschooled in Russia through the sixth grade)

George Bernard Shaw — Irish playwright and outspoken socialist (b. 1856; irregular schooling due to his own hatred of organized schools)

Matthew (Mattie) J.T. Stepanek — Poet and writer, especially about peace (b. 1991; taught at home until his death at the age of 13 in 2004 from a rare form of muscular dystrophy)

Jason Taylor — Professional football player; best known as #99, defensive end for the Miami Dolphins (b. 1974; homeschooled at least throughout high school)

Mark Twain — Prolific writer and American satirist best known for *Tom Sawyer* and *Huckleberry Finn* (b. 1835; some schooling before 1847, but his writing education began only after he left school and apprenticed with his brother, the printer)

Mercy Warren — Influential Revolutionary War writer (b. 1728; no formal schooling at all, but she was allowed to use her brother's tutor's library)

Booker T. Washington — Former slave and scientist known as the founder of Tuskegee Institute (b. about 1856; although he attended schools after he was freed, I am including his name on this list because he initiated all educational contacts himself and thus provided for his own education from a young age)

Phyllis Wheatley — Poet and extremely gifted writer around the time of the Revolutionary War (b. about 1753-1755 in Gambia, Africa; tutored by her owners because no other option was open to her as a slave)

Woodrow Wilson — 28th U.S. President during the First World War (b. 1856; home educated by father because of the Civil War until he entered Princeton in 1875)

Andrew Wyeth — Artist known for rural depictions (b. 1917; educated entirely at home after the third grade and chose to home-school his own children, including Jamie, when talents became evident – see http://www.nfgcc.org/51.htm)

James Browning (Jamie) Wyeth — Artist known for personal paintings of people and animals (b. 1946; son of Andrew Wyeth; left public school in the sixth grade to be tutored at home and devote more time to art)

Many of these famous people considered school a waste of time. There are a number of quotes to this effect by such prominent people as Winston Churchill (whose own schooling was sporadic), Benjamin Franklin, Andrei Sakharov, Albert Einstein (often on the lists of the home educated but omitted here because of the number of school experiences he had), Mark Twain, and others that are a part of the public record. Of those who wished they had attended more school (such as Abraham Lincoln and Booker T. Washington), it is apparent that their efforts to make up for their 'lack' of education contributed largely to their successes as adults.

Self-education is a hallmark of home education for many older kids, and is seen as a sign of success by many home educators. This is because all of us are truly self-educated, if you think about it. Education is a personal journey that we must be actively involved in. There are many well-taught people who never became very well educated, because they allowed themselves to fall into the passive learner trap. The best educated people I know are self-motivated in learning no matter how they are educated, and the people selected for this list certainly qualify.

"Is it legal?"

Yes, in all fifty states, and it has been since 1993. It has never been illegal in some states, although the requirements vary drastically from state to state. It is vital to know the laws in your own state to home-school. Fortunately, there are many sources where the laws are clearly explained. If you would like to see specific state regulations in greater detail, they can be found at www.hslda.org (or www.hslda.com). Just click on the word homeschooling on the toolbar near the top. That will help you get in touch with what your state requires.

Here is a brief explanation of options available in different states, though. There are only a few types of legal models for home education. Sometimes homeschools can be defined as very small private schools. If the families comply with the private school laws of that state, then they can teach their own children at home.

Some states regulate homeschools as a separate category of school, and the requirements vary significantly from state to state where this is the rule. However, the regulations are usually spelled out adequately, and home educators have been following these statutes successfully for many years.

Another option is for home educating families to associate with a private or religious school, which can oversee the homeschooling process or regulate the requirements for each homeschool as a 'satellite' of its campus. This type of private or religious school can be called an 'umbrella' school, because it provides legal shelter for the homeschool. Many are accredited by local and state accrediting agencies. Umbrella schools notify their member families of required regulations, which are usually clear and easy to follow. That makes them a popular option.

Occasionally, homeschools are operated under a religious exemption from public schools. Exemptions are becoming less necessary as home education gains more legal ground, and are usually only one of several options in a state. There are other varia-tions of these options as well, and most states allow more than one option within their borders.

"What exactly does the law require?"

Since homeschools are regulated mostly by state laws, laws vary significantly from state to state.[8] Some states require very little, while others have burdensome requirements that keep home educators bogged down in paperwork. However, there is no state whose requirements are so burdensome that no one has decided to teach their children at home there. All states have home educators.

While it may seem like a good idea for the state to make sure home educators are teaching their children well by imposing lots of regulations, current research shows no difference in the achievement of home taught students in states with greater regulation versus those in states with less regulation.[9] In other words, more rules do not give better results than fewer rules. Here is what various states have required, have tried to require, or currently require, in no particular order (Remember – these are from the laws of all fifty United States – no one state requires all of these, and some of these requirements are from an either/or list of options):[10]

- Notice of intent to homeschool
- Application for permission to homeschool
- Apply for religious exemption from compulsory schooling
- Notice of attendance, filed regularly
- Instruction for a given number of hours per day, a given number of days per year
- Teaching must occur during comparable public school hours
- Yearly evaluation by a licensed psychologist
- Submit to yearly physical exams
- Submit immunization records
- Teach for the prescribed number of hours at "the regular home school location"
- Curriculum must "be structured and based on educational objectives as well as the needs of the child, be cumulative and sequential, provide a range of up-to-date knowledge and needed skills, and take into account the interests, needs, and abilities of the child"
- List of curriculum choices for the year
- Notification of specific, personal information about students being taught
- Have the same school year length as public schools
- Use of an approved correspondence course
- Maintain minimum scores above a certain percentile on annual testing (sometimes as high as 50th percentile – the "middle child" on the achievement scale)

- File Individualized Education Plan (IEP - for autistic children) to school system along with certification of disability
- Consultation with a three-year home school veteran
- Include a log of reading and other materials used
- Must teach in the English language
- Inclusion of certain subjects in the yearly curriculum (some of these lists are extensive and detailed, including such subjects as substance abuse, traffic safety, fire safety, patriotism and citizenship, the nature and effects of alcohol, tobacco, and narcotics, agriculture, hygiene, disease control, first aid, conservation, in addition to obvious academic choices like reading, writing, and arithmetic)
- Submission of grades or narrative evaluation of each subject on a quarterly basis
- Yearly approval of curriculum choices
- Yearly testing, or at other regular intervals
- Certification of at least one parent
- Bachelor's degree, High school degree, or GED for at least the teaching parent
- Oversight by a certified teacher
- Submission of yearly portfolios (i.e., examples of a student's work in each subject)
- Home visits

As you can see, some of the regulations seem arbitrary or burdensome, while others seem reasonable. Depending upon the number and types of these regulations combined in a state law, any state can be described as having "high", "moderate," or "low" regulation. Since there is no statistical difference in the achievement of students in states rated as high, moderate, or low regulation, high levels of regulation seem pointless.

Recent research[11] also indicates that previously home educated adults are happier, more active in their communities and government, and more satisfied with their jobs than those who weren't homeschooled. Since these are children who grew up before many of the high regulation states adopted their restrictive laws, it is a reasonable guess that regulation does not necessarily correlate with social adjustment, either.

"How are you accountable?"

See "What does the law require?" in the previous section for examples of specific regulations we have to follow. However, I have to say that our greatest source of accountability is ourselves. We enter the home education arena with the intent to improve the lives of our children, and know that we will have to live with the consequences of our choices. Unlike classroom teachers who pass children on to the next teacher each year, parents face the same children year after year. Thus, if mistakes are made this year, we and our children have to deal with them the next year, so it is to our advantage to correct any problems as they arise.

There are also large homeschool communities in almost every city now. In the earlier years of home education, homeschoolers were more likely to be 'lone rangers,' doing their best in isolation. That is now an unusual situation. There are home education conventions and curriculum fairs, tutorial classes, community programs, support groups, and other opportunities to get to know other people who learn at home. The home education community as a whole tends to be pretty tight-knit and helpful. Struggling parents have many sources of help to turn to. In my circle, most of the home educators I know have gently nudged other parents to consider changing one aspect or another of their program. Most regularly ask for help from others, too.

"Do you have to test the kids?"

In some states, yes, and in others, no. Many parents who home educate in states where testing is not required do it anyway to keep abreast of their children's strengths and weaknesses, or just to teach their children how to take standardized tests. Some parents choose not to have their children tested, since they are able to assess their children just fine without them. When you are working one-on-one with your children daily, it is pretty obvious what they know and what they don't. Their strengths and weaknesses are no secret. While tests are not the best way to assess a student's progress, I know very few parents who are surprised by their children's test results.

My personal bias is to have them tested, because whether the tests tell *you* much or not, many people will indeed judge your children based on tests results. Thus, they need to have experience taking tests. I view annual testing as a class in taking and scoring well on tests. However, that is exactly what it is — a bias. There are many reasons to exempt children from the trend toward rampant testing as well.

"Where do they get tested, and who tests them?"

Some children are tested at home by their own parents, in the same environment where they learned to make the scores as relevant as possible. Some parents, however, want their children to be tested by someone else to ensure the highest level of objectivity, so there are many options for this. Many home education umbrella schools provide testing for the students registered with them. Also, many public and private schools allow children in their districts who are taught at home to test with them, sometimes for a fee. Finally, parents can ask a certified friend or hire a teacher to do the testing for them. Tests can be ordered online or through catalogs from testing services, which grade the tests and prepare the reports. These are all valid ways to obtain test results to fulfill most state testing requirements.

"How do they do on national tests compared to publicly and privately schooled children?"

Very well, actually. In fact, homeschoolers consistently outperform both their publicly and privately schooled counterparts on standardized tests. This is true even when you consider that one-fourth of the children are enrolled one or more grades above their assigned age-grade level, and often take tests designed for older students (Rudner, 1999). On other measures of achievement, like college entrance exams, they are also very competitive. Homeschooled students scored an average composite ACT score of 22.6 (out of 36) in 2004, while the overall national average was 20.9. [12]

More significantly, the racial and gender-related achievement gaps that have persisted in public schools are greatly reduced or absent in available homeschool statistics. In a 1997 study by Dr.

Brian Ray, white and minority students across all grades had identical reading scores, and only a five-point discrepancy in math scores. There was no significant difference between the achievement of boys and girls, either[13].

Homeschooled students won the National Geography Bee in 2005, 2003, 2002, and 1999, while at least one home educated child finished in the top three most years. In 2005, 12.5 percent of the 273 national finalists in the Scripps-Howard National Spelling Bee were home educated, and a homeschooled child tied for second place. Home educated students finished in the top three places in 2005, 2003, 2000, 1999, and 1997. In 2000, all top three finishers in the Spelling Bee were home educated, and so were two of the top three finishers in the National Geographic Geography Bee. This was an extraordinary year for homeschoolers, but there are almost always home educated students represented somewhere in the top three spots in these and other national contests, including medical, court, debate, technical, and other competitions. When it is not uncommon for 33 percent or more of the top finishers in national contests to come from 2-4 percent of the population, it's time to think that there must be something special about that population.[14]

"Is there any research on homeschooling? What does it say?"

Yes, there is research. I have summarized a few studies, not necessarily in order of their publication. There are many more studies than the ones I have chosen, but it would take a whole book just to summarize them all. I have tried hard to choose a representative sample of research.[15]

Before I list these studies and some of the conclusions reached in them, I need to make a point. Most of the results you will see in these studies make home education look good. This is not because I am selecting only those studies that favor home educators, but because most studies simply DO reflect well upon homeschools. I have specifically sought out studies that showed the weaknesses of home education, and have found only one that was specifically critical in side-by-side comparisons with other educational options, and that one openly stated that the graduates studied were not typical homeschoolers in any way.[16] Although there are editorial statements that clearly reflect negatively on homeschooling, such as the National Education Association's (NEA) unsupported assertion that "home schooling cannot provide a comprehensive education experience,"[17] those and other opinion pieces cite no research for me to look up and provide for you here. Here are overviews of some representative studies:

1.1 Million Homeschooled Students in the United States in 2003 and Homeschooling in the United States:1999 by the U. S. Department of Education (USDE)[18]. These are two national surveys from a program conducted periodically, and are the latest that collected information on home educators. Although questions were not the same, it is interesting to see the responses side-by-side. The information from the 1999 survey will be more complete, since its entire 30-page report is available, while only a research brief is available for the 2003 survey. Here are some of the findings of both surveys:

- In the spring of 1999, the USDE estimated that 850,000 students were being homeschooled – the equivalent of 1.7 percent of the school-aged population. In 2003, the estimate grew to 1,100,000, or about 2.2 percent of the school-aged population.
- In 1999 some characteristics of homeschooling families were collected. In that survey, 75 percent of homeschoolers who responded were white (non-Hispanic), compared with 65 percent of the general population. The household income of homeschoolers was comparable to that of non-home-schoolers. Home educating parents had higher levels of educational attainment than non-homeschoolers. Home educated students tended to live in more two-parent families with more children at home than non-homeschoolers, and more of the families lived on one income. The 2003 survey did not address these demographic issues.
- Both the 2003 survey and the 1999 survey questioned parents' reasons for homeschooling. The reasons were similar in both surveys. The most popular reason given for choosing home education in 1999 was "Can give child a

better education at home" (48.9 percent of respondents chose this), although many reasons were included to choose from. The 2003 number one pick was "Concern about environment of other schools" (31 percent of respondents). The second place reasons were similar, too: in 1999 it was "Religious reasons" (38.4 percent), and in 2003 it was "To provide religious or moral instruction" (30 percent). Other reasons provided for home educating included: 1999 – "Poor learning environment at school" (25.6 percent), "Family reasons" (16.8 percent), "To develop character/morality" (15.1 percent), "Object to what school teaches" (12.1 percent), "School does not challenge child" (11.6 percent), "Other problems with available schools" (11.5 percent), "Student behavior problems at school" (9.0 percent), "Child has special needs/disability" (8.2 percent), and "Other reasons" (22.2 percent). Parents could select more than one reason in 1999, and there were other specific choices with very small percentages of response. Only a few choices were given in 2003, and parents were asked only for their main reason rather than all reasons that apply. Here is a summary of the 2003 responses: "Concern about the environment of other schools" (31 percent), "To provide religious or moral instruction" (30 percent), "Dissatisfaction with academic instruction at other schools" (16 percent), "Other reasons" (9 percent), "Child has a physical or mental health problem" (7 percent), "Child has other special needs" (7 percent).

<u>Scholastic Achievement And Demographic Characteristics Of Home School Students In 1998</u> by Lawrence Rudner of the College of Library and Information Services at the University of Maryland. According to the abstract, this was "the largest survey and testing program for students in home schools to date" (abstract, p. 1), including over 20,000 students in almost 12,000 families. It includes a review of test results and a parental survey. The respondents were all contacted from the same testing source, Bob Jones University Press Testing and Evaluation Service, so there are some problems associated with that. Bob Jones University Press is affiliated with a fundamental Christian viewpoint, and has a history of

racially divisive actions. Because of that, minority families and non-Christian families may not have chosen to use Bob Jones in representative numbers. With that in mind, demographic characteristics based on religion and race are almost certainly skewed, so I did not include those results in this summary. Since those who used this testing service may also have used the Bob Jones curriculum and the teaching methods associated with it, this probably doesn't equally represent all the methods and curricula associated with home education. So, where I say home educators in describing the results of this study, I really mean, 'home educators in this group.' Otherwise, this study gives a very comprehensive picture of this group and has many good points based on objective test results and survey responses. Here are some of them:

- Home educated children watched considerably less TV than other children.
- The median[19] amount of money spent per child per year was $400, although parents reported spending as little as less than $200 to more than $2000 per child. Home educators in this study had higher average incomes than the national average at the time, with more than half making between $36,000 and $75,000 per year [Note: this is in contrast with the 1999 USDE findings, above].
- About 77 percent of homeschooling moms did not participate in the work force, and of those who did, most worked part time. This compared to about 30 percent of mothers with children under 18 nationally. About 97 percent of homeschool parents were married couples, compared to 72 percent of parents of school-aged children nationwide.
- Almost one out of every four homeschool students (23.6 percent) had at least one parent who was certified to teach. There was no significant difference between the test scores of the children of teachers and the children of non-teachers, however. The average level of formal education achieved by home educating parents tended to be higher than that attained by parents nationwide.
- Home educators had more children than the national average: about 65 percent of homeschool families had three or

more children, while only about 20 percent of families nationwide had more than two children.

- Nearly one-fourth of home educated students were enrolled one or more grade levels above their age-peers. They outscored their publicly and privately schooled peers in every subject at every grade level, and those who had been homeschooled the longest outperformed their group-schooled peers by the greatest margin. There was no significant difference in the achievement of homeschooled girls and boys at the fourth or the eighth grade level. [20]

Home Educated and Now Adults: Their Community and Civic Involvement, Views about Homeschooling, and Other Traits, a 2003 study by Dr. Brian D. Ray.[21] This particular survey questioned adults who had been homeschooled for seven or more years between Kindergarten and 12th grade, and summarized social trends in adults who had been home educated compared to the general population of adults. One thing to note – because of the relatively young 'age' of the modern home education movement, most of the adults surveyed for this study were young adults (78.6 percent were between the ages of 18 and 24), with nearly half still in college. This, of course, will affect the results when comparisons are made to older populations. Here are some of the findings:

- More home educated adults between the ages of 18-24 had taken college classes than the general population that age (74 percent compared to 46 percent).
- Home educated adults read more books and magazines, and watched less TV than the national average.
- Home educated adults were more involved in ongoing community service, joined more community organizations, visited public libraries more often and attended more religious services than the national average.
- Home educated adults were far more involved in political campaigns and activities, and voted much more regularly than the general population (for example, 76 percent of 18-24 year old home educated adults had voted in the previous five years, compared to 29 percent of 18-24 year olds nationally.).

- Home educated adults scored higher on all measures of personal happiness – sometimes at a rate of 2:1. They were twice as likely to rate themselves as "very happy," found life more exciting, and were more satisfied with their work and incomes.
- 95 percent either agreed or strongly agreed with "I am glad that I was homeschooled," 92 percent agreed that having been homeschooled was an advantage as an adult, and only 4.4 percent said they were not likely to homeschool their own children.
- Of the adults surveyed who had children aged 5 or older, 74 percent were already homeschooling their own children.

Home Schooling: From The Extreme To The Mainstream by Patrick Basham of the Cato Institute. This 2001 study was published as an occasional paper of the Fraser Institute in Canada. Since it is a review of other studies, I will not discuss specific 'findings.' However, this is a good overview of home education in general, and is recommended reading for those trying to find out more about home education. It covers a number of the issues that most concern parents considering the practice. It also has a great bibliography, which makes it a wonderful place to start more in-depth study.[22]

Endnotes for chapter 6:

1. This quote was from chapter 3, retrieved online at http://www.sntp.net/ education/school_state_3.htm
2. This was obtained from http://www.dvschool.org/psngatto.htm, which was linked from http://www.preservenet.com/theory/Gatto.html
3. Alden, 1998; available at http://nj.npri.org/nj98/05/prussian.htm.
4. As cited by Karl M. Bunday in his Schools and Crime FAQ on http://learninfreedom.org/School_makes_crime.html
5. Alden, 1998.
6. Published in 1964 by Pitman Press.
7. Better Late Than Early was published by Reader's Digest Association in 1989 but is currently out of print. Dr. Moore has written many other books as well, including School Can Wait, Home Spun Schools, Home Built Discipline, and Home Grown Kids.
8. An easy source of information on the laws of your state can be found at

the Home School Legal Defense Association (HSLDA) website at www.hslda.org or www.hslda.com.

9. Ray, 1997.

10. All the regulations listed came from a compilation of the state laws as described on the HSLDA website.

11. From Dr. Brian Ray's study entitled *Home Educated and Now Adults: Their Community and Civic Involvement, Views about Homeschooling, and Other Traits.* Available through the National Home Education Research Institute (NHERI) at www.nheri.org.

12. According to the ACT website (http://www.act.org). The ACT is a test given to juniors and seniors in high school to determine academic readiness for college.

13. This is true both for the 1997 study by Dr. Ray, available at http://www.hslda.org/docs/study/ray1997, and the 1999 study by Lawrence Rudner, available at http://www.hslda.org/docs/study/rudner1999.

14. Some other indicators of home educated children's academic achievements can be found at http://www.hslda.org/docs/nche/000010/200410250.asp.

15. Other sources of current research are at the A to Z Home's Cool website: http://geocities.com/nelstomlinson/research.bibliography.html and the Home School Legal Defense Association website at http://www.hslda.org/research

16. A discussion of that 2004 study is found in the "All Grown Up" chapter at the end of the book, and is called *Final Analysis of Evaluation of Homeschool and ChalleNGe Program Recruits* by Wenger and Hodari. I accessed it from http://www.cna.org/documents/D0009351.A2.pdf

17. NEA resolution B-69, 2004.

18. Both of these were conducted by the National Center for Educational Statistics (NCES), which is a division of the USDE.

19. Median is a statistical term that means middle, when you put all numbers in order.

20. This is not the case in public schools. According to the 2003 Nation's Report Card, girls scored significantly higher in reading, and boys scored slightly higher in math.

21. The results I am quoting are from the HSLDA synopsis of this study called Home Schooling Grows Up. Dr. Ray is the President of the National Home Education Research Institute (NHERI), and has conducted a number of studies to date. You can obtain the results of his full-length study and his other studies at http://www.nheri.org.

22. This paper can be viewed at http://www.hslda.org/research, and originates at www.frasierinstitute.ca.

Socialization

"I'm afraid my kids won't be socialized adequately if I homeschool."

It's funny how often home educators are asked about socialization, and it's on every interviewer's list of questions. Socialization is of primary concern for those who educate their own children, too. A 2003 survey by the National Center for Educational Statistics[1] asked respondents for their main reason for homeschooling. 31 percent responded that the social atmosphere of schools was the primary influence on their decision. The respondents said, in effect, that they were homeschooling *because* of the improper socialization that occurs in schools, not *in spite of* missing out on social opportunities offered by schools. They believed that the socialization of their children would be better at home than in school.

According to Webster's New World Dictionary, "socialized" means: "to adapt or make conform to the common needs of a social group; to subject to governmental ownership or control...", and that seems to fit the socialization we often see in our schools today. It also reflects the history and purpose of public education in this country (see "When did homeschooling begin?" for more details).

"Conforming to the needs of the social group" is not necessarily a good thing. Although children must learn to conform in group settings when appropriate and called for, this does not take precedence over other social skills, and these are not learned by taking a class. These skills must be learned by practicing them frequently.

Children need to be guided by those who can help direct and shape behaviors individually, not in a group. Opportunities must be available to practice these skills in a wide variety of settings.

This type of opportunity is not available in most schools. The social setting found in schools is just that – found ONLY in schools. Nowhere in the adult world have I daily found myself in a group situation segregated by age, geography, and ability. Home educated students can spend their days with people of various ages and abilities, and are not overwhelmed by peer pressure. Although they have virtually limitless opportunities to spend time with age peers, they do not spend the *majority* of their time *under the influence* of those peers. Children who have the opportunity to be around people of various ages learn social skills from those who are older and more experienced than they are. They practice those skills in a very wide variety of settings while supervised and while unsupervised. Thus, they learn the skills to get along with a variety of people in our diverse culture by participating in the culture. I think that's what most of us really mean when we talk about making sure our children are socialized.

According to the 2003 survey *Homeschooling Grows Up* by Dr. Brian D. Ray,[2] previously home educated adults are happier, more involved in social activities, more likely to pursue higher education, and more likely to be involved in the political processes in our country. Dr. Ray also found in *Home Education Across the United States* in 1997 that the average number of regular activities engaged in by homeschooled students was just over 5, and that 98 percent engaged in two or more activities. Older research also praises the social benefits of home education. According to Professor Larry Shyers' 1992 Doctoral dissertation, the homeschooled students he studied showed fewer behavior problems than group-schooled peers, and were similar to schoolchildren in self-concept and assertiveness. This is in contrast to earlier research by Professor John Taylor who, in 1986, found that home educated students had considerably *higher* self-esteem than their age mates in school. Professor Thomas Smedley concluded in 1992 that home educated students were more mature and better socialized than group-schooled children. Dr. Raymond Moore found in 1986 that home taught children were "happier, better adjusted, more thoughtful, competent and sociable children."

Also in 1986, Professor Mona Delahooke concluded that home educated students were less peer-dependent than private school students, and that they were at least comparable in social and emotional adjustment. It doesn't sound like homeschooled kids are missing out socially, does it? These and other studies support my belief and experience that home education can provide excellent opportunities for positive socialization of children.[3]

"Won't it make them different?"

The basis of this question is often rooted in plain old-fashioned fear. Many people are afraid of 'differences.' They are afraid that if their children are not in the same type of educational setting as all their friends, they will look different. This leads to two different fears: 1. that other parents will ostracize them for having children who are not the same as theirs, and 2. that other children will shy away from their children.

So – here is my response to that. Differences are nothing to be afraid of. Yes, some homeschooled students can be different or unconventional at times, but that is not a bad thing, as long as it is not criminal or immoral. Is this the test of what is right and good – whether or not it conforms to the 'standard' set by others? That's just peer pressure, and it's a hard habit to break, even for adults. If your children are well-behaved, well-educated, and happy, why should you care what other parents think? Most home educated students are very capable of moving appropriately in a wide variety of social settings, so occasional disapproval is simply a chance for them to practice budding social skills and prove their detractors wrong, as they usually do.

Parents are sometimes afraid that being educated differently will affect their children's abilities to make friends. If that is your worry, don't. As mentioned earlier in my response to the 'socialization' question, home educated children have a good record for acquiring positive social skills. Children tend to model their behavior after the people they spend the most time with. If you're not too weird, they won't be, either. It's always a good idea to find a number of good role models for your children, whatever age they might be, and if those people behave admirably, your children will, too.

That's another advantage of home education; you can go out of your way to find opportunities for your children to be around those who will support good behavior, and limit the time they have to spend with those who behave anti-socially. That doesn't mean they won't come into contact with those who behave badly, because they couldn't escape it if they tried, but they won't spend large amounts of their time under the influence of anti-social peers. You can help them process difficult situations calmly as they arise without forcing them into overwhelming situations on a regular basis. This is a good recipe for encouraging confident, friendly behavior.

"Aren't you afraid your children will grow up to be closed-minded?"

Yes I am, and that's one reason why I home educate. Those who are protected and taught at home are perfectly aware of their protected status, and that is easily remedied as they grow. Children who receive a religious or conservative education are constantly exposed to secular and liberal thought. It is on every television and radio station, every government pamphlet, and nearly every billboard. They could hardly avoid it if they tried. On the other hand, it is entirely possible to progress through the educational institutions in this country without encountering deeply religious or conservative views intelligently expressed.

Those who are publicly-schooled rarely realize how protected they are from any deep consideration of views that counteract the political positions that dominate our schools. If you ask the typical non-religious, politically liberal person to describe a person who only went to very conservative religious schools from preschool through graduate school, they would probably say that person was closed-minded. If you ask the same person to describe someone who only went to liberal, secular schools, on the other hand, they probably would not appreciate how narrow that education can be.

The news is full of stories about legislatures, school boards and school systems in dispute over controversial ideas that one side or the other will not allow to be presented *in addition to* 'approved' positions in public schools. Most of the approved views are based on liberal political ideology. Teachers who try to discuss politically conservative or religious perspectives in a non-judgmental way are fighting an uphill battle, and students are losing out in the fight.

This is true at the university level, too. A 2005 article in the Washington Post cites a few numbers. "By their own description, 72 percent of those teaching at American universities and colleges are liberal and 15 percent are conservative..." That's a *five-to-one* ratio. The most telling comment in the article, after giving statistics to show how religious and conservative faculty are not present in large numbers on campus, was, "It's a very homogenous environment..."[4] The gap was widening in recent years, too. From an article in The Daily Texan that cites even higher ratios: "The implications of these realities are obvious - there has emerged a culture within the academic system in which only one set of ideas is believed and discussed. This has dangerous implications for the spirited debate so central to education."[5] I want my children to be exposed to liberal political thoughts that are intelligently expressed. I am simply asking for the same consideration to be given to other types of thought. I want them to be engaged in truly spirited debate.

"Someday your kids will have to face the real world."

For children taught in the context of the community, that day is every day. They have to confront the reality that messes made before school don't mysteriously disappear during school, and get to see how much groceries really cost. They interact with a greater variety of people in their travels throughout their communities than the average child sees while in school. The insides of more community resources become familiar as their parents take them places to help 'round out' their educations. They spend their lives in the real world.

Of course, you may mean that someday children will have to face difficult situations. Some people who don't teach their children at home must think that home educated children have a perfect life, with no problems, where all social situations are artificially engineered to prevent unhappiness. That is not the case. There are problems in every human relationship on the planet. Just because homeschooled students rarely have to deal with recurrent bullying problems does not mean that all their relationships are perfect. Home educated children can't hide their difficulties with siblings, peers, and neighbors when they are in small groups with them often. They HAVE to work them out. Even if they wanted to, parents could not prevent relationship problems from occurring. They are simply a normal part of life. Children don't have to experience overwhelming hardships in order to be prepared for the real world. They just have to experience life.

"You can't protect them forever."

Protecting children is not such a bad thing. Parental protection is necessary for healthy development and a secure childhood. We all prevent our toddlers from crossing streets by themselves because they are unable to recognize the dangers there. We can all agree that two-year-olds need more supervision than 17 year olds (Well, MOST 17 year olds!). The problem is deciding on the timetable that determines when children are to move from protection to mentoring. That timetable is not, and should not be, the same for all children.

It is a very recent trend to universally separate children from their parents at the tender age of five. This is not entirely based on the development of children. According to a 1994 Early Education and Development article, "There is…little empirical evidence to suggest that age five is necessarily the optimal age for school readiness. While there is little to suggest that age five is optimal for readiness, there is less to suggest that some other age might be better. In fact, it has been proposed that arbitrary restrictions on readiness as a function of age are misdirected efforts at imposing a rigid schedule on widely varying child development (NAEYC, 1990)."[6] Parents are in a unique position to know when *their* children are ready for certain freedoms and responsibilities, and home educating parents can release their children in a gradual way that reflects their development in a variety of areas over time. That way, children are ready for the challenges of life as they come.

I believe that the issue is not that most home educated children are overprotected, but that most group-schooled children are underprotected. Our smallest children are simply not prepared to become one out of 20, and to deal with all the problems and ideas they have to face in school. They *need* their lives to be simplified for them. Instead, many are presented with overwhelming and often conflicting social agendas pushed on them by 'progressive' teachers. Six-year-olds are just not ready to mediate the cultural clash that is occurring between school agendas and parental values. It's a tragedy that they are in that position at all.

Middle school children are still not mature enough to deal with many issues. When I was teaching during the Gulf War I followed a developmental guide to discuss the war with my sixth graders. One warning it included was that sixth graders would be afraid of being personally hurt. Since I had a high opinion of my students and believed them to be well-informed about the War, I thought the guide was not giving them enough credit. However, when I asked them for questions and comments, their main concern was that Iraqi planes would bomb Nashville, TN, where they lived, and particularly *their homes*. That was developmentally right on target, even though logically it did not make sense to me as an adult. Basically, it reinforced the truth that sixth graders are not adults. They need deep and controversial topics to be presented to them in small, appropriate packages.

Our oldest children, while not being protected enough in some ways, are being overly limited in others. Many teens are segregated from the world at a time when they could be most useful to others. They are prevented by their schedules from getting out into society and working in the internships and apprenticeships that will prepare them for their future lives, and will help them see how academics apply to the real world. Their social consciousness is at its peak. Many teens have a wonderful tenderness for others and an optimistic desire to change the world. Unfortunately, that energy is often sucked into an endless cycle of band practice, football, tutoring, and other self-oriented activities. The opportunity to develop that social consciousness is often lost or the focus is turned inward. What a shame.

They also have to deal with social issues that are much more prevalent in the unreal social atmosphere of schools than in the rest of life, such as pressure to cheat, flirting and acceptance of promiscuous behavior, generalized peer pressure, drugs, alcohol and partying, and inappropriate antisocial 'pranks.' When they have nothing useful or relevant to fill their days, teens will fill their days with alternatives to relevant and useful activities. Many of these pressures start bad habits that last through a lifetime.

The voice of experience and good judgment needs to be louder in our children's lives. When home educators are accused of over-protecting their children, they are usually doing what I believe all parents should do – reducing (not eliminating – that's impossible in today's culture) the overwhelming level of 'noise' our children have to sort through on a daily basis. I believe that this component of home education is the very reason why we have children who are so confident and sure of themselves – they have been given the time and the tools with which to process the input in their lives in an orderly way.

"Don't kids need to be around other kids their age every day to grow up well adjusted?"

In most of the world, it is more important for children to be well grounded in their families than with other children to be well adjusted in that culture. The family is nearly always charged with preparing children to fit into society, in whatever way that culture dictates. Forcing children to spend their entire lives as part of an age-segregated group is not healthy, and is not necessary to become socially well-adjusted adults. This philosophy comes from the early roots of compulsory education in this country, which strove to strip children of their individuality. Keeping them in these groups is essentially the same as expecting children to 'socialize' each other.

Age-peers *are* an important part of growing up, as are friends of all ages. However, they are simply a part of the tapestry of friend-ships available to children. Children who spend the majority of their time with other children their age depend more on their friends than on better sources for information and support. How many teens do you know who will weigh the advice of a friend more heavily than that of a parent or dependable adult when they need help, if they tell the parent about the problem situation at all? This is common, but not logical. I'm not saying children need to tell their parents everything, or that they shouldn't have deep, intimate friendships with peers, but the unreasoning neediness we see in our children for age-peers is acquired. I think our society systematically trains children to depend upon the approval of their peers. This is not the case in all cultures, and many societies have better adjusted children than we do.

"How do they learn to get along with others if they're at home all day?"

They are *not* at home all day. Even homebody home educators have 'forays' into the world. Shopping is necessary for all families, and most take part in some of the endless variety of options available to them: homeschool support groups, trips to the library, church events, community activities, politics, sports, art or music classes, movies, boy scouts or girl scouts, 4-H, community theater, … the list goes on and on. People learn to get along with people by being with them, AND by having guidance in what is proper behavior by those who have experience in proper behavior. You can't learn to get along with others without both of these elements.

Fortunately, these are both available to home educated students. The perception that homeschooled students are somehow 'cloistered' at home all day is inaccurate. The environment they experience is more real and bigger on average than schools can provide. Home educated children experience life more as adults do, including getting along with a variety of people – not just with children their own age.

"What about the prom, senior trips, and other activities?"

Yes, there are homeschool proms, as well as other dances and 'normal' social outlets. They simply have to be organized. Hmmm… that sounds like a good exercise in organizational and life skills for a group of juniors in a homeschool support group. Of course, if they don't really want to organize one, there are often others in their communities who have already done so. Some things *can* be a little harder to do in homeschooling, because someone else hasn't already done all the work for you, but that mirrors real life a little more accurately, don't you think? I think it's good that not everything comes easily – not everything has been done for you. Our family sought out a group that already had experience in organizing things like dances, and other social experiences, which made those things easier for us.

But, that's what people do in real life, isn't it? Find resources when available? That's a valuable life skill in itself.

The prom question makes it clear to me how deeply ingrained the school perspective is in the parents of today. In frontier towns, the question would be, "How can we come up with good activities for our children?" This would elicit a variety of answers from the diverse members of the community who all probably had different opportunities as children and young adults. The task then was to sort out the best suggestions and to make them work.

Today, parents seem to be asking how they can reproduce their own experiences for their children. Parents are reluctant to branch out for fear that what they provide won't be as good as what other kids get. That seems to me to be a direct result of our own experiences with school. The teacher always has the 'right' answer, and if our answers don't match it we might get 'bad grades.' This mindset stifles many inspirations.

Thankfully, however, many home educating parents are breaking out of that mold, and are finding a level of freedom and creativity they previously did not know was possible. Some examples of senior 'rites of passage' that I have heard of and known are: a trip as a group to Stratford, Ontario, to see the Shakespeare festival; trips to Washington, DC, or to other parts of the world; seniors who put on and participated in social events in the context of charity; a senior fashion show; all girl dances (This was a Muslim alternative I heard about); a formal 'tea'; charity fund-raising dinners; the list could go on and on. We have enjoyed some unique and fun activities. Purim costume parties (Purim is a Jewish festival in which people dress up and reenact stories from Esther in the Bible) and an English Country Dance (like the dances in the movie *Pride and Prejudice*) are only two.

Many young people experience many of these and more. The only limits are the imagination and personal preferences. I am thankful that there are a lot more choices out there for my children than the prom, although they are welcome to participate in a prom, if they choose to do so.

"Can homeschooled graduates participate in graduation ceremonies? Can they get yearbooks and class rings?"

Yes. In fact, the ceremony can be tailored to fit the exact preferences of the graduate and her parents, if desired. Many umbrella schools and state homeschool organizations arrange graduation ceremonies for their members, too. Our children will probably graduate with other students from middle Tennessee through the Middle Tennessee Home Education Association[8], since many of their friends will attend that ceremony. I attended this ceremony to support former students, and it was beautiful. All the trappings of a formal graduation were there, including caps and gowns, diplomas, speeches, and music, but there were some extras, too. Each of the two or three hundred graduates had a table highlighting his or her accomplishments, and pictures of the appropriate graduate flashed above the stage while each student accepted his or her diploma. It was a very memorable experience.

Some graduates prefer a more individualized approach, though. Graduation can be as large or as small as you wish. It is easy to design a small personalized ceremony when you don't have to coordinate many schedules. Any proposal can be considered; when you are doing all the planning, you don't have to follow someone else's format.

Graduation invitations, gowns, class rings, and other 'typical' senior items are readily available on the Internet[9]. Yearbook kits can be purchased, too, that will help 'novices' create their own yearbooks. Many umbrella schools, support groups and homeschool tutorials create yearbooks for their members, and students are usually involved in assembling them. These and other trappings of graduation are just details that *represent* the substance of a student's accomplishments. However, they are fun and can be provided with minimal effort.

Endnotes for chapter 7:

1. The National Center for Education Statistics, or NCES, is a branch of the United States Department of Education (USDE).

2. *Homeschooling Grows Up* is a synopsis of a longer study by Dr. Ray called *Home Educated and Now Adults: Their Community and Civic*

Involvement, Views about Homeschooling, and Other Traits. Available through the National Home Education Research Institute (NHERI) at www.nheri.org.
3. An article that condenses these findings is found on the HSLDA website at http://www.hslda.org/docs/nche/000000/00000068.asp.
4. Kurtz, 2005.
5. Burnham, 2005.
6. Crnic and Lamberty, 1994.
7. MTHEA has a website at www.mthea.org, for more information.
8. Josten's has a homeschool page at http://www.jostens.com/homeschool, as one example.

Academics and Teaching

"How do you know what to teach?"

How do other schools know what to teach? I would never have thought to include death education as a formal class in my child's schooling, but that's an option – or a requirement – in some schools. Many subjects are at the discretion of the parents, especially in elementary school. Most topics are pretty easy to choose, like reading, writing, and arithmetic. Science and social studies are also pretty standard at some point. All of these can be tailored to the needs of the younger child. At the high school level, there are usually very specific requirements for high school credits in order to qualify for graduation. A list of these can usually be obtained from a local school board, an umbrella school, or a state home education organization. Then, all that remains is how to meet those requirements.

This is actually easier than it seems, because there are many sources of curricula that meet and exceed the state standards for each required subject. At that point all you have to do is what it says in the teacher's manual. Most of the high school students I know who have been home educated for any length of time know how to work through material pretty independently. This is evidence that home educated students are doing what their parents had worked to teach them how to do; they are learning how to teach themselves. This is an important skill for college. Also, many community colleges are stepping in to cover high school subjects that require labs or other difficult courses. While these were often designed to meet the remedial needs of unprepared college-age students, they have been very helpful to many high school students as well. Another source of curricular requirements comes from curriculum suppliers who have had to meet state standards.

Many suppliers have comprehensive curriculum choices, and these choices can guide the parents into what to teach. I have listed a few curriculum suppliers in the appendix, if you would like to look at some available choices.

"What about the hard subjects?"

You mean, like calculus? If your child is interested in calculus, then the chances are that either you, your spouse, or both of you have some smarts in that area, as the apple really doesn't fall far from the tree. On the other hand, my children constantly amaze me with what they can do, and I am sure they will pass me up soon. There are several options available in that case.

First of all, most community colleges offer classes for high school students, and those are a good option for upper level high school classes such as calculus or particle physics. Distance courses on the Internet or video courses are also available from homeschool providers and universities trying to meet these needs. These are usually good options for classes that are best taught with expert input when no experts are available, like Spanish or British Literature.

Another option that is increasingly available to home educated students is the homeschool tutorial. A tutorial is where parents hire a number of tutors to get together in the same place at the same time and offer classes in their specialties. These can be college preparatory classes, or simply classes most requested by parents in the home education community, like art, band, and sign language. Most are a combination of the two.

Another option, when a parent is simply not comfortable teaching a given subject (usually a non-essential one) or feels the need for reinforcement, is the homeschool cooperative. This is where home educating parents get together one or two days each week and take turns teaching classes of interest to the other families in the group. For example, I might teach math or sign language, while someone else might offer crafts or creative writing.

As you can see, there are many alternatives for parents who want extra reinforcement for difficult subjects. The key is simply to stick with it and find a way to meet your child's needs. This can-do attitude becomes a lifestyle for most home educators. When the education, and therefore the future, of your children rests squarely on your shoulders, you become focused on doing whatever it takes to provide your children with the best that is available to you. It's very effective, too.

"How do you handle grading? How can you be objective?"

Before I start describing how I grade my children, I'd like to briefly discuss why letter grades exist in the first place. 1. When a teacher has a room full of students, it is important to keep track of how each child is doing in each subject. Grading helps the teacher remember what objectives each child has mastered, and keeps her from confusing one child's achievement with another's. In theory, it also lets the teacher know when to move on to the next skill. 2. Grades tell the child how he or she is doing in comparison to a set standard, but also in comparison to other children. 3. In addition, many people outside of the classroom want to know how a child is doing: the parents, the principal, the district that tracks school achievement, funding agencies, colleges, the athletic director, etc. So, grades help the teacher to inform others of how each child is doing in an easily recognizable way. In this section, I will focus on letter grades. To see the discussion of other ways to evaluate student work, see the next section, labeled, "How do you grade subjects that you teach unconventionally?"

It is not necessary to use grades to decide whether or not a child has mastered a skill in an intimate homeschool setting most of the time. Mastery is obvious. Since you don't have lots of new students to keep track of, and they are not all doing the same thing, it's not that hard to tell who knows what. If you do have trouble keeping track of what each child has completed, letter grades are not the only way to do so. A mastery checklist based upon the curriculum you are using or the skill you are teaching works just as well. Knowing what to work on is not hard to see, either. If your child stumbles over certain syllables when reading aloud, that's what that child needs to work on. If your child consistently gets the right answers in math, she probably can go on to the next topic. If not, you should work on the current topic before moving on. It's really a common sense approach. For this, letter grades in the traditional sense simply are not necessary. Many home educators do not use them for this purpose at all.

The worst use of grades is to compare one student to another. This is not necessary for most of the elementary school years. Why? Because the child who does well can be satisfied with his or her accomplishments without having to feel that he or she is doing better than others are doing. It is enough to know that mastery has occurred. When comparisons are introduced or are emphasized, the child who does well tends to focus on those comparisons instead of the intrinsic value of the work being done, and sometimes feels superior as a result. That is simply human nature. It's not very noble or useful, though. For the child who is not doing well, comparisons can be devastating. There is nothing like working hard for academic gains, then finding out that the child in the seat next to you did twice as well with half the effort. How discouraging that can be!

Grades do not serve advanced or remedial students well at all, and have little purpose for the average student. They distract from the real purpose of learning – satisfaction in accomplishment and in mastering necessary skills. According to Alfie Kohn in High School Magazine, "...study after study has found that students — from elementary school to graduate school, and across cultures — demonstrate less interest in learning as a result of being graded."[1] Many home educators do not use grades for the day-to-day achievements of their children for these reasons.

Sometimes there is the need to communicate a student's mastery level to those outside the educational setting. Some state laws require home educators to report grades to some reporting agency, like the school system or an umbrella school. This is an imperfect system, but it is common and convenient, and it is the law. In this case, the most important part of this question is, "How do you grade your children *objectively*?" Some subjects seem easy. In math, for example, you simply arrive at the percentage correct and translate that into a letter grade using a set grading scale, right? Well, that's certainly one way to do it, and many people use this method. However, this goes back to our reasons for using grades at all. We want to communicate to others the mastery level our children have achieved, right? What if I don't let my children move on until they have mastered ALL of what I have presented to them? They will always get 'A's.' I try to present to them only relevant work that is developmentally appropriate for them, without wasting their time with busywork, or discouraging them with inappropriately difficult work.

Here is how I 'grade' their written bookwork. If they get something right, I put a check mark next to it. It is 'checked off.' It is done. If they don't, I leave it blank or circle it so it is easy to find – it is *not* 'checked off.' It is not done. They have to go back and correct whatever mistake they made, with extra instruction if necessary. If ten percent or more of their work contains errors, we approach it again from a different angle. That way, I know that whatever they have studied they know well, and they are prepared to go on to the next level. So, my children have mastered everything I have taught them at the 90 percent to 100 percent level, and they have at least demonstrated that they are able to get the correct answer on their own one way or another at the 100 percent level. They don't go on until they do. If I make a mistake and offer them work that really is too difficult for them under those conditions, that's not their fault, so why should they suffer poor grades for that? That's a teacher error, not a student one. Remember, the purpose is to have children who really learn – not to have those whose grades 'make you proud.'

So, grades can't be very objective under these circumstances. Unfortunately, grades aren't much more objective in a school setting. Student grades are often more of a reflection of the instruction they receive than their achievement. Students either suffer because of the poor instructional decisions that have been made for them, or they benefit from the insight and capable instruction of a perceptive teacher. This does not always reflect mastery of material. Sometimes grades simply reflect a child's emotional state on the day of the test. The real point of grades is to reflect *mastery* to someone else, not just the ability to answer specific questions when required.

"How do you grade subjects that you teach unconventionally?"

This is a really good question, and it shows that you know that not all home educators teach out of workbooks and give them written tests. It goes back to the purpose of grades – to communicate to others how a child is doing academically. There are many ways to do this, if you think creatively.

One popular method to use is the portfolio. A portfolio is simply a collection of student work that reflects his or her skill level in a particular area, usually over a period of time. This is a tool often used by artists to display their work. It works quite well for students, too, and shows progress very effectively. In fact, this method of evaluation is required by some state laws. This is a particularly effective way to compare writing samples over time, or keep records of items that reflect a child's development.

Sometimes you don't need to use grades, and that can bring a lot of freedom in the instructional realm. For example, if your older child is extremely interested in animals, he or she may do an internship at the local veterinarian's office. In that setting, your child may assist in surgeries, help with billing, learn how to groom and care for certain animals, and help with research into unusual animal conditions for the purpose of diagnosis. Often a child in that type of real-life setting gets interested in a certain aspect of the work, and spends hours outside of the volunteer office researching that aspect – like helping animals with certain ailments, for example. So, he or she forms a hypothesis about that condition, and tests it at work.

That is extremely useful learning, right? How do you grade something that you are not directing, though? Something that has no specific set of educational objectives at the outset? Grades in a setting like that don't mean much, but a lot of valuable learning is going on. Occasionally, though, the learning in this type of setting needs to be recorded and evaluated to comply with state laws. In cases like this one, an anecdotal record (like a journal, or 'log', of what is done) is useful and sufficient for the purpose of keeping track of educational experiences. Older children can take care of this requirement themselves, with oversight by the parents.

"How do you teach several children at a time – especially at different age levels?"

Good question. In a group setting like school, there is usually a teacher who directs the learning process, typically teaching everyone the same thing at the same time. This is a model that was designed for efficiency – one person can impart knowledge to many students at once. This is not the only way to teach, even for 'schoolish' home educators. Here are some ways some home educators may teach more than one child at the same time:

- Older children (about middle school age and up) can work independently while younger children work with parents. Since younger children don't need very long to learn the basics each day, there is still plenty of time to work with older children on more difficult concepts. Younger children can begin to learn the basics of self-directed learning, too.

- Teenagers can manage much of their own day-to-day instruction. Some may use video or computer courses that are self-instructing, others may take correspondence courses that expect independent work, while others may simply be disciplined learners. Other teens learn about life in a less textbook-oriented way. Helping them to become self-directed long-term is an involved process, but it is very rewarding. In this type of situation, parents become supervisors who only step in when things are not going well. Teaching young people to be self-directed learners is not the same as telling a teen to do his work and leaving him at home all day. Teens still very much need their parents' input. Parents of these marvelously independent teenagers are continuously involved in the planning and implementation of education for these older children, but sometimes more as mentors than teachers. It is important that parents understand that self-instruction is not a skill that develops naturally with age, but with practice and incentive.

- Many subjects can be taught across age levels with very little modification. For example, who says five-, eight-, ten-, and eleven-year-old children can't all learn about the Middle Ages at the same time? It's actually pretty easy to teach children to listen to read-alouds together, especially if you are reading novels about a time period or culture. The younger children simply play with math manipulatives or other silent, non-interactive toys while Mom or Dad reads the story, and then everyone can talk about what happened together. It makes for a pretty fun way to learn, actually. Then, projects can be done, if desired, at different levels of proficiency. This method works pretty well for subjects such as science and social studies. Enrichment topics, such as music and arts and crafts, can also be done together.

- Often, older children can help younger children with specific concepts, or can help to reinforce topics already taught by the parent. For example, while I am working with one child, another of my children might be reading to siblings about a subject they are studying. Or, one of my younger children might read out loud to one of my older children. There are many ways children can constructively get involved in one another's education, and I believe it is beneficial for all involved. Because of this experience, my thirteen-year-old daughter had the confidence to start teaching a younger child in the community to play piano when she was only eleven, and she did very well. My twelve-year-old daughter can interact with children of any age, and has a lot of 'tricks' up her sleeve to keep younger children interested in what she is doing with them. This skill will serve her well.

"How do you deal with toddlers and infants while you teach older kids?"

There are lots of ways parents can 'deal with' (I think 'engage' is a better word) the youngest members of their families and still get things done. Here are some of the ideas I have used or heard over time:

- Teach older children during naps or snack time.
- Have older children take turns occupying the youngest children while the other children are 'doing' school.
- Keep a special box for the times when you must have focused time with older children: Toddlers may only open it

then and explore its contents, which change regularly. Some parents keep 5 boxes – one for each day. Or – plan a special activity once each day for the little hands while older children do other work.

- Let the toddlers sit on your lap or take part with older children while you teach. This builds patience in older children, and prevents some of the behavior problems that happen when a small child feels left out. Be forewarned, though: your younger children may learn skills you thought you were only teaching to your older kids. My youngest daughter learned to read at the age of two while sitting on my lap as I taught an older child to read. Being involved in family educational activities gave her a hunger for learning that has not diminished over time.
- Use a playpen for certain times of the day.
- Swap 'services' with other parents one or two times a week – they watch your little ones while you tutor their children in an area of your strength, and vice versa.
- Utilize a Mother's Day Out program.
- Teach older children more within the context of real life during this season of your life; i.e., use activities you would already be doing to teach basic skills. For example, teach math to your seven or eight year old when you go to the grocery store. Make him figure out the tax on your purchase, or keep a running total of the cost of the trip as you go along, or subtract each item from the amount of money left, thus keeping a running total of what's left. Have him read the labels on the food, or look for certain brands. Have him look for warning labels on certain foods, like saccharin packets. You get the idea. Other academic skills can be taught or reinforced with cooking, reading aloud, doing projects that require reading, etc.
- Teach your older children to be more independent in certain areas of their lives. Thus, you can be more flexible with the time spent with your younger children.

"What about children with special needs?"

As a certified special education teacher and the mother of four children, I can say without reservation or hint of doubt that ALL children have special needs. As a parent, I am in a unique position to know those needs intimately and to respond with love. As a teacher, I can say that even well-trained, experienced teachers don't always have it all together and know all the answers regarding special needs. They rely heavily on the input of parents.

Of course, I am aware that you are asking about those children with certifiable handicapping conditions or giftedness. To many parents in the position of nurturing a child with more intense needs, the thought of home education can be a daunting and overwhelming one. And, there is a good reason for this. Homeschooling in those conditions should be considered carefully before jumping in. It is not appropriate in all circumstances to try to do everything yourself. Home education *can* be an excellent option for exceptional students, however. It is flexible, individualized, does not lend itself to constant comparisons and is consistent over time. Students taught at home do not have to adjust to different teachers each year or every few years.

Group schooling targets average students. Those who don't 'fit the mold' often lose something when put into a group education situation, but special students can shine in the individualized environment found at home. Other parents must agree with me, because in 1999 parents reported that they were homeschooling 69,000 students *because* of their special needs.[2] There are a lot of resources available for parents of children diagnosed with special needs.[3]

Let's start by talking about gifted students. In one study of home educated students' standardized test scores, one-fourth of homeschooled students were taking tests designed for students one or more grades above their assigned grade level, and were still outperforming public school students by 30 or more percentile points on average.[4] In other words, they skipped or progressed more quickly through one or more grades.

Why aren't there more kids in school who are skipping grades? Perhaps schools cannot offer gifted students the opportunity to accelerate in the same way homeschools can, or maybe more students are capable of accelerating and performing well than are identified in schools. Maybe parents of accelerated children are choosing to home educate in record numbers. Who knows? I think all of these factors and probably some others come into play. Many parents either remove their children from school or never send them at all because they see a lack of challenge for their bright, inquisitive children in the school system. It is much easier to provide children with materials and opportunities to explore their areas of passion at home than it is in most school settings.

For example, I have a child who loves bugs. He always has. Because of his interest, he is always reading about them, catching them, collecting them, drawing them, and talking about them. This interest led him to challenge himself in reading in a way that school 'readers' never could. This same child has never been good at sitting down, although he is getting better. Until the age of eight, he tended to struggle with studying anything for longer than ten minutes. Then, he began to be able to stretch that time out and get more done, especially in math, which is one of his strengths. Because of his birth date, my son would have been in second grade and studying grade level materials at the age of eight.

However, I can assure you that would not have been productive. By the time he was officially in second grade, he was starting third grade math. He enjoyed it and progressed quickly through it. He was not reading at a second grade level at the beginning of second grade, though. He is now beginning fourth grade and reading at the seventh grade level or so. When he was ready to progress, I simply gave him the materials he needed to go on. He could be challenged individually in a way he could not in a class with 20 other students. In school he would have had to struggle through reading material he wasn't ready for at the beginning of the year, while at the same time not being challenged in math. He might have labeled himself as dumb or as a 'bad' reader when he compared himself to those who had learned to read earlier, even though he was perfectly normal. He may have learned to not work hard in math, which is a bad habit that has crippled many talented students.

All of these things hamper a student's progress in the long run. Individualizing in this manner would have been very difficult to do in a school setting. First, it is nearly impossible to keep kids from comparing themselves to each other. That makes it difficult to assign vastly different levels of schoolwork to different kids, not to mention the organizational and supervisory nightmare that would cause. Second, accelerating a child by having him skip a grade has its own issues. Most accelerated children are not uniformly accelerated, so skipping a grade may set a child up for failure in a specific subject or in the age-segregated social setting found in school. In an individualized setting, it is possible to accelerate a student only in the areas where it is appropriate to do so, and the child can still interact with others in a developmentally-appropriate way.

Extremely gifted students have unique issues as well. Many show characteristics of 'problem' children in school systems, including restlessness, extreme independence, distractibility, knowing answers without being able to explain processes, and many more.[5] These children need a type of individualization that may not be available in a regular school setting. So, home education can be a good and flexible option for gifted and accelerated students.

What about the student with certifiable handicaps? Well, the same benefits that accrue to gifted children work for those with handicapping conditions as well. In fact, parents report that some milder learning challenges seem to disappear when they bring their children out of a group situation and into a one-on-one tutorial. Some children diagnosed with ADD and ADHD stop using medication when they begin their education at home. Children often become much calmer and less stressed when they stop attending school. Children diagnosed with mild learning disabilities in early grades may find that their areas of weakness actually become their strengths as they enter the higher grades, as those areas were focused on in their individualized programs at home. Children thrive when they are not constantly comparing their learning styles to others, and often develop very creative minds. That is not the case for all children with learning differences and difficulties, of course. Many children still need medication or additional intervention. But, in general, homeschooling is a good option for children with mild learning problems.

Those with more significant learning issues are a challenge, too. The children with Down Syndrome still have Down Syndrome, those with autism still have autism, and those with cerebral palsy still have cerebral palsy when homeschooled. How do they do? Let me answer that in a story. My first experience with a homeschooler with a handicapping condition was when I was working as a house parent in a group home for adults with autism in the early 1980's. One of the adults there had an extremely determined mother who had set up a structured environment for her son in the basement of their home, where she taught him throughout most of his childhood after removing him from school. He achieved far beyond the 'basic self-help' levels predicted for him by his former schoolteachers. He was one of the few adults there who could read at all, looked people in the eye when talking with them, and was unusually capable of taking care of himself as compared to the other residents. Was he still autistic? YES! He was still very handicapped. However, he also was extremely well prepared for the environment he entered as an adult, which is the goal of most home educating parents. His mother had a greater vision for her son than his teachers had, and chose to take things into her own hands for her autistic son in an era before home education was accepted even for non-handicapped students. What she did was clearly very difficult and time-consuming, and I certainly would not expect most parents to choose this route with their exceptionally handicapped children. It may not even be the best option for all children. However, she did a great job, and her son benefited greatly from it.

For those willing and able to educate their handicapped children at home, I just want to say that it is possible. Individualization is extremely effective for all children, but especially important for those with handicapping conditions. Many parents who choose to teach their children with special needs at home also take advantage of some of the services offered by the school systems or private providers. Physical therapy, occupational therapy, speech therapy and other specialized services are essential for many children. The goal is to provide the best possible educational services for each child, and sometimes that takes more than one provider.

Although I have heard some people grumble that home educators should not be allowed to 'pick and choose' which services they accept from the school system, I have to ask, "Why not?" Home educating parents pay the same taxes other parents pay — the government to whom they paid those taxes simply does not always pass on that money to the school system. That places an unfair burden on the schools that provide the services.

Some schools have asked parents to pay a fee to make up for lack of public funds diverted to their child, while others have proposed asking federal programs to provide part-time funds for students with special needs who utilize special services. Since special education programs are bursting at the seams in most big districts, this could offer a solution that is beneficial to all.

"Can kids get all the same courses at home that they could get at school?"

Urban home educators usually can get all the classes they need either at home or in the community. This can be a concern for those living in rural communities, where there are not as many opportunities on a community-wide basis. The costs of some programs can be a factor for all. However, creative home educators can usually get the information they need in some way or another. A library card with inter-library loan privileges can do some amazing things! Mail order materials can cover just about everything under the sun, and the Internet has opened up a whole new world for home learners and teachers.

I know of several home educators who homeschool *because* the local schools don't offer all the classes they need, especially higher-level classes for accelerated students. Many schools don't offer classes like Calculus, intensive art programs, or the wide array of Advanced Placement (AP) classes some students need to prepare for the programs they want to pursue in college. These are classes that can be offered at community colleges and in distance education programs though many universities. So, in some cases, learning at home is the *only* way they can get some courses.

"Can homeschoolers really get as good an education at home?"

Research indicates that they can definitely get a better academic education, and both research and anecdotal evidence suggest that most prefer it. I have looked through mounds of data while preparing to write this book, and have hunted for research that compares children who learn at home with children who attend school. The outcomes significantly favor home educated children. Overall, children who learn at home excel in academics, social skills, civic involvement, individual sports, extracurricular activities, and other arenas of interest to them.

That does not mean that all opportunities are equal when compared to schools, however. In artistic pursuits, home educated students clearly have an advantage. They have more time to pursue their interests and obtain apprenticeships. In athletics, though, many high school and college sports programs require extra tests and paperwork to allow homeschooled teens to participate in local leagues and school teams, if they are allowed to participate at all. This is due mostly to outdated fears and stereotypes, which is changing. The National Collegiate Athletic Association (NCAA), which previously required homeschoolers to submit tons of paperwork and get a GED[6], has recently streamlined the application process.[7] Now home educated athletes simply submit evidence that they have successfully completed a high school program, including standardized achievement tests scores similar to the ones taken by all other high school students, to participate in college athletics. These are basically the same requirements as for other high school seniors, which is a major victory for college-bound athletes.

Many of the difficulties students taught at home face come as the result of external and artificial barriers erected by the non-home educating community. Some problems are sponsored by powerful political lobbying organizations with a vested interest in public education, like teacher's unions. For example, when Tennessee passed lottery legislation in 2003 and decided to offer college scholarships to high school students using monies from the lottery, legislators had to decide upon standards for eligibility. The standards they originally came up with required higher ACT and SAT test scores from home educated students than from public school students, rather than having a universal standard for all students. That has since changed, but each change brings with it new hurdles to overcome. Athletic associations geared toward public schools have refused to allow home educated students to play on school teams, and some have gone so far as to penalize public school teams for playing homeschool teams even in scrimmage, or unofficial, games. Fortunately, this is changing, too. Entire leagues of homeschooled students are forming, and almost any high school sport is now open to home educated students in some form or another. The trend is moving toward all schools competing on more equal footing.

"How do you homeschool high school kids?"

That depends on the laws of your state. It is essential to be aware of any specialized state regulations for high school. The first step, of course, is to see what's required by your state for graduation. That information can be found on the Internet from your state Board of Education or from a state home education association. After that, there are several options different families choose. Which of these options they choose, of course, often depend on the aspirations, talents, and temperament of the student in question, as well as the skills of the parent.

Some people choose to 'go it alone' by putting together their own curriculum based on state standards. This can be a good option for fastidious record-keepers, and isn't as difficult as it sounds, with the abundance of home education materials available to choose from. It simply requires that there be some support for the difficult subjects, either from the curriculum provider or from community sources. Most cities and many smaller communities now have a large homeschool population. It's not uncommon for parents to enter bartering agreements with each other and community resources to get support. In other words, if you help my kids with calculus, I'll help yours with term papers. Or, if your church will provide space for our tutorial, our support group will keep your building clean.

Other students may choose to get a high school degree through a distance-learning program. These are increasingly offered by colleges and universities that are invested in attracting well-educated applicants who are familiar with their programs. Some are well established, and new ones are springing up all the time to meet the demand. Some programs are completed entirely online, while others require some or all materials to be sent in and graded. Again, which program is chosen depends upon the nature of the student and parents in question.

Another option is to enter a tutorial program where you can pay other people to teach certain subjects in their areas of expertise. A 'tutorial,' when described by homeschoolers, usually means a day or two of group classes each week with paid tutors. This is convenient, because this makes more courses available with a smaller time commitment for traveling than other options. It is also less expensive than arranging for individual tutors for children. These are becoming more popular as more people choose to teach their children through high school. Still others enroll their high school age students in a community college for a joint or dual enrollment program.[8] This often will allow them to get some college credit while still attending high school.

<u>Endnotes for chapter 8:</u>

1. Kohn, 1999.
2. According to the US Department of Education National Center for Education Statistics 1999 survey.
3. Some good sources of information are found at the National Challenged Homeschoolers Associated Network –NATHHAN website: http://www.nathhan.com and at the National Foundation for Gifted and Creative Children website: http://www.nfgcc.org
4. Rudner, 1999.
5. For more information on school's influence on gifted and talented students, see http://www.nfgcc.org/c.htm which is a page on the website for the National Foundation for Gifted and Creative Children. This particular page details the founders' experiences with school for their highly gifted child. The index for this site is found at: http://www.nfgcc.org/htmindex.htm.
6. GED stands for <u>G</u>raduation <u>E</u>quivalency <u>D</u>iploma. Students can get this by taking a test. This process was designed to give adults who did not finish high school an opportunity to demonstrate that they had high school level skills. It was not designed for college-bound students.
7. See this article by the Home School Legal Defense Association called *NCAA Eliminates Waiver Process For Homeschoolers.* at http://www.hslda.org/docs/news/hslda/200402/200402090.asp
8. *Joint* enrollment usually means taking college level classes at the same time as high school classes, while *dual* enrollment means getting both high school and college credit for the same class.

Materials, Cost, and Extracurricular Activities

"Where do you get your curriculum?"

When home education resurfaced in this country as a significant movement in the second half of the last century, there was not a lot of choice in curriculum. Parents could either get a few books from programs for Christian schools or missionaries, or could use what the public schools used. That wasn't a lot of help for the parents who were teaching their children at home because the public school curriculum wasn't working for their child.

Now, by contrast, curricular choices can be overwhelming. You can still use the old choices, but there are also numerous programs developed just for the home education market. Home education catalogs are plentiful, and homeschool supply stores are popping up all over. Just do an Internet search for 'homeschool supplies' and you'll quickly see what I mean. Most large booksellers such as Barnes and Noble and Books-A-Million also carry some home education materials, as well as many Christian bookstores. Mainstream Internet sources, such as Amazon.com and eBay, are also popular with home educators who know what they are looking for. And of course, there is the old standby – the library. More and more libraries are carrying titles for home educators, and lending libraries or collections aimed especially at homeschoolers are showing up in cities around the country.

Another common source for homeschool materials is a local curriculum fair. Each year state and local homeschool organizations host gatherings where curriculum venders and homeschoolers get together in one place at one time. They frequently offer seminars on relevant topics and materials, too. These fairs are often held in the spring or summer, and are usually advertised in local newspapers, on official state websites, and in even in libraries. They provide a great opportunity to see what new products have been released in the past year, meet other local homeschoolers, and to learn about subjects of interest to you.

Used curricula are widely available, too. Used book sales are very common, and are usually advertised anywhere support groups are (local libraries, on the Internet, local churches, and through state homeschool associations). There are numerous websites and message boards devoted to selling used homeschool materials, and those are easily found by searching the Internet.

"Is your curriculum as good as the ones in public schools?"

For my purposes, it's better. Public school curricula are designed for, well, public schools. They specialize in group lessons when I need individualized instruction, and use too many artificial materials, like fake money, when I have access to the real things. They also tend to reflect the agendas and goals of the school lobbyists, and are often plagued with extreme political correctness, sometimes at the expense of rigorous academic standards. Most of the curricula I use are designed for use with individuals and if needed, use materials found in the real world. Real coins and bills, recipes and assembly instructions, and real books serve us better than textbooks in many subjects, although we also use excellent textbooks designed for homeschooled students. The choices are virtually endless.

There are home educators who get rid of textbooks altogether and use alternate methods to teach their children useful skills. That is, they use books from the library to teach their children to read, objects in their environment to teach their children to count, and use real-life experiences and interests to teach their use in the world. Shopping, building things, and that sudden interest in a topic covered on the History Channel or in a book they read qualify as school. So, not everyone uses textbooks and chalkboards to teach their children practical skills. Education does not require a curriculum, but there are some good ones available for those who choose to use them.

One major advantage home educators have over schools is the ability to admit mistakes in purchases. When I taught in schools, textbooks were chosen by a committee for an entire school system or for a single school. Teachers had to use texts listed among the 'approved' choices, regardless of the students enrolled in their classes. In addition, if they found they had the wrong book, it was a terrible process to get rid of the old texts and acquire new ones, which may or may not be better or help the current class of children. Texts had to be ordered by the set, and something that worked for one child might be disastrous for the next.

In contrast, if a book is not working for a particular child at home, the parent can chuck it and get a different book in short order, tailored specifically to meet *that* child's needs. So, for *that* child, the risk of having materials that are boring, inappropriate, or simply poorly designed is greatly reduced. I use more than one math curriculum, for example, because what worked well for one child didn't work as well for another. Two of my children use one math program, while two use another, all on different levels. I have the freedom to choose methods and materials that met each child's specific needs. Thus, for *my* children, the materials we use are better than the ones found in schools.

If what you want to know is if children taught at home are demonstrating knowledge that is equivalent to that of children in other school situations, the answer is a resounding 'yes.' As diverse as our materials can be, what we use is working better than what the public schools use when test scores are used as an indicator. However, that is not the only indicator. Students who learn at home, in my experience and in studies, are also more likely to use their skills in their everyday life and in their communities. That, in my opinion, is a far better indicator of the effectiveness of the materials used.

"Is homeschooling expensive?"

It can be, but it doesn't have to be. It's kind of like a choice of cars – some people choose the top of the line sports cars, while others drive used minivans. In Lawrence Rudner's study, most home educators spent between $200 and $599 per child per year on home education in 1998. I assume that the *average* has gone up some in the seven years since then, but that reflects what I've spent every year before this year. Some home educators do pretty well with the investment of writing materials and a library card, and spend far less than average. I have expensive years and less expensive years depending upon our needs and circumstances, and have spent between $50 and $600 on educational materials per child in any given year. I use a relatively expensive curriculum, but since most of it is reusable and I have four children, it's a pretty good value. This year I will be spending an all-time high on two of my children who are in a tutorial, and will spend over $3000 on their classes and materials alone. However, since I will be reusing materials for my other children, in all I will average about $875 per child this year. That's about $1550 for each of my older children, and $200 for each of my younger ones. That's pretty inexpensive for an individualized program, considering that I spent over $300 the year I had two kids in 'free' public schools trying to get required materials and keep up with all the mandatory fund-raisers, etc.

Let's consider the costs of some of the other choices, too. Private schools can run from a meager $2000 per child for church-subsidized religious schools to $25,000 or more per year for exclusive independent schools and boarding schools. Public schools spent from a low of about $6,000 per student for independent charter schools to a high of over $16,184 or more per year on each student, in 2001-2002.[1] Where does it all go? Why don't average public school students do *ten* to *eighty* times better on standardized tests than average homeschooled students, or than private school students in less expensive schools, for that matter? Why don't they get better jobs or have fewer emotional problems with an investment like that? I guess that just illustrates the fact that the investment of money in education is not the best way to produce results; it's the investment of more important things in each child that matters.

"How do you know if your curriculum's working for you?"

How do you know if the car you bought is right for you? It

works. How can you tell if it works? When you try it out, it feels good, it responds predictably, etc. Well, it is the same with home education. When it's working, you see things beginning to happen that you want to have happen. For example, your children begin to have those 'aha' moments that show that they understand what's going on and make it all worthwhile. When you discuss the book that your child just read, she seems to understand what the main point was. When you are helping your children with new math concepts, they either have that telltale blank look, or they attack the new concept with vigor. When you're teaching a child one-on-one, comprehension is obvious. And, if it's not working, it's not too difficult to change the materials and approach you're using to improve the odds.

Of course, there is always the testing that is so prevalent today. Homeschooled students do very well on standardized tests as a group. Even though I have used test results to compare home educated students with other populations throughout this book, it's not the best way to tell if a student is doing well. The test may not have had any questions about a trouble spot, thus inflating a score, or, conversely, the test may cover concepts you have not taught that year, thus deflating the score. Usually there's a combination of those two factors. In home education, test results usually produce no surprises, and, when they do, it is usually better to trust what you see on a day-to-day basis.

Extracurricular activities:

Exceptionally talented children often need to pour more time into their gift than is available in a school schedule. For example, a gifted swimmer who goes to school might get up at 4:00 AM and swim from 4:30 AM until 6:30 AM, then go to school, swim again for 3 hours after school, then eat and do homework before going to bed. While there are some motivated teens willing to do this every day, this is a hard life for anyone. Since home education is very efficient, a high school program can be covered in fewer hours most days than in school with no transportation needed, and a youth can spend the same five or six hours per day training with down time scheduled into his or her life. This is important to both the athlete and the family. On the other hand, some parents worry that their musically gifted child may not get a chance to participate in a band if home educated, or wonder if their outstanding football player needs time on a school team to develop his skills and get noticed before college. These are valid questions and concerns, so I have tried to address them here.

"What kinds of sports opportunities are available to homeschoolers?"

In the elementary years, most areas have community leagues for most team sports. Urban centers would also have ice rinks, tracks, and other facilities where students can hone their skills and pinpoint their interests. Local chapters of the YMCA often offer homeschool gym classes, and many regions will have other options for the athletic elementary school student. In junior and senior high, the options are more limited, but usually available to the motivated student. More and more umbrella schools are offering sports to their enrolled students, and some public and private schools open their doors to home educated students in their districts, although often with some restrictions or strings attached. There are currently competitive alternatives to school programs in all sports with the possible exception of football, and support for creating competitive football programs is growing. These alternative programs, including the Amateur Athletic Union (AAU)[2], are open to students from any educational background.

Since the schedules of home educated teens tend to be more flexible than those in schools, some students find that home education allows them more time to pursue their interests. Many athletes are taught at home to allow them time to practice and focus on their sport – particularly individual and paired sports such as tennis, gymnastics, skating, and so on. As home education communities grow in urban centers, homeschool leagues are also popping up for team sports such as basketball, baseball, soccer, football, and others.

Home educated students now have the same requirements as any other high school graduate when competing for college scholarships. "In early 2004, NCAA [National Collegiate Athletic Association] streamlined the process for homeschoolers and the good news is that homeschoolers no longer have to go through a waiver process as non-high school graduates. Homeschoolers now go through the same process as other high school graduates."[3] The key, as always, is preparation. If your athletically talented child wishes to compete for college scholarships, then research requirements. If your child wants to play on a team, find out what teams are available in your area. If none exist, perhaps it is time to form one, or gather support for a high school team so one will be available for your child when she is old enough to participate.

"Do homeschoolers have access to art programs?"

Art is available in many forms to the home learner. Local art museums often offer programs for home educated and other students though community outreach programs. Community programs such as the YMCA have taken an interest in providing art for elementary school students. This is a popular class to offer through home education cooperatives and tutorial programs, too. There are also a number of art programs offered for the student to study at home. Video courses, books, and art materials are available in every homeschool supply catalog. An apprenticeship or work study program can make a nice addition to a homeschool art program for the motivated student. There are many artistic home educated students who thrive in the homeschool environment, because opportunities to create are not limited to certain times of the day or to the particular talents and interests of a school's art instructor. As with other extracurricular activities, artistic pursuits are aided by the flexibility of scheduling and the efficiency of instruction afforded by home education.

"What about performing arts, like music and/or drama?"

Most musically inclined children take lessons, no matter where they go to school. Exceptionally talented youth need extra instruction, guidance, and outlets, however. Many communities have homeschool bands, and some public schools will allow students in their districts to participate in extracurricular activities. These types of arrangements usually require some kind of compromise on the part of the home educated student, however, such as part-time school attendance. Many urban centers have music and drama activities available to interested members of the community. More and more have daytime classes, as the demand for them has grown. Many children take advantage of flexible schedules to pursue parts in plays, apprenticeships in local symphonies, bands, choirs, and other opportunities. There are also churches with wonderful choirs, drama programs, and other outlets for young people to participate in. The main advantage to the musically or dramatically talented child provided by learning at home is the opportunity to participate in activities NOT specifically designed for children. They can audition for productions that may practice during school hours or simply require too much time for most children with homework. The motivated home educated child can complete schoolwork and still have more time available for this sort of activity.

"I enjoyed being in clubs in school. Are there any open to homeschoolers?"

Sure. Most community-based clubs are open to any students, regardless of where they are educated. Some are more common in schools, but all clubs had to be started at one time or another by someone who was interested in doing so. So, my advice to you is to start a club if your choice is not available to you now. Many churches and community gathering places will allow you to meet there, although there may be some restrictions. There are lots of good clubs ready for you to join. Most groups are not exclusively for homeschooled students, but there are some that are, often because of scheduling issues. Although they may meet at schools, they are usually not school-sponsored and are therefore open to home educated students. Some examples are: Boy Scouts, Girl Scouts, 4-H, chess clubs, Young Republicans, Young Democrats, AWANA, Keepers at Home, Girls in Action and Royal Ambassadors, Pioneers, Reenactment clubs, robotics teams, debate, quilting groups, MathCounts, Forensics, etc. There are many, many more, and remember – you can always start your own to fit your interest, if needed. Advertise a little, and you'll probably find others who share your interests.

Endnotes for chapter 9:

1. Johnson, 2005.
2. Information on the AAU can be found at this website: http://aausports. org
3. See *NCAA Eliminates Waiver Process For Homeschoolers* available from http://www.hslda.org/docs/news/hslda/200402/200402090.asp

Qualifications of Parents, and Religious Reasons for Homeschooling

"Are parents really qualified to teach their own kids at home?"

Are they qualified to raise them at all? What makes a person qualified to do anything? There are no guarantees that anyone is. There is a point where we just have to start with some basic assumptions if we are to have any freedoms at all. Sometimes we try so hard to prevent mistakes that we also prevent genius. While I believe that some parents are probably not qualified to teach their children, that is based more upon character issues than upon the educational issues that usually produce this question. In my opinion, parents who are hard-working and motivated to learn and teach, devoted to their children, and flexible in their approaches are generally qualified to teach their children at home. Extra regulations will not improve upon that, and 'safeguards' like teacher certification are not magic bullets. We all know of certified teachers who operate classrooms with no evidence of common sense, while there are grandmas who have a gift for relating to children and getting a concept across. As a tutor for children in school situations, I was constantly amazed at how simply paying attention to a child would raise his or her achievement, even when I was asked to tutor in fields outside of my expertise.

Relationships are the first priority in any teaching situation, and parents are uniquely qualified in that area. Parents tend to have similarities with their children that allow them to understand their thought processes better than strangers would. For example, I know why my daughter has to run her hands over everything in the world that has texture, because I do that, too. So, as far as the teaching relationship goes, parents definitely have the advantage over paid professionals.

You were probably asking about academic qualifications, though, right? Can parents teach calculus and debate when the time comes, and what about that really important task of teaching reading? Can parents do a good job of that? Let me reassure you about the reading part. Teaching reading is a lot easier than potty training, and more pleasant, too. There are so many available programs designed to teach reading that parents can't escape finding one that fits their situation. Most are pretty easy to use. You just have to follow the directions, and in some you just have to read the words written in red. The same is true for most early elementary subjects. So, if you aren't the type to research a topic and come up with your own methodology, don't worry. That work is already done for you.

In my experience, the only difference between materials written for home educators and those written for schoolteachers is that homeschool materials tend to have much better written directions for the teacher. Since home educators are very picky about having high quality materials that are easy to use and they spend a lot of money, suppliers are constantly rewriting, revising, and updating materials. The choices are getting better all the time. Materials for schools, on the other hand, are often reviewed more for political correctness than ease of use. As a certified teacher I've had experience with both.

As for the higher level subjects, very few parents rely on their own expertise for all subjects. Most look for other avenues for their children who need help in high school subjects. By the time children reach the high school level, they tend to be self-learners in most subjects, and are ready for more personal challenges. In centuries past, most qualified children went off to college sometime between the ages of 11 and 16, when they were ready to study higher levels of materials under people who were not their parents. Since that is not an option today (college programs are no longer geared toward intense mentoring relationships with young people), high school age children can branch out into distance learning courses, video courses, tutorial programs, community programs, community college courses, apprenticeships, intense self-study or some combination of these or other options.

This approach is not only more flexible, it requires a more active role on the part of the students. We want our children to actively participate in their own educations. This is ideal, because their educations can be tailored to fit them as needed, and they can learn the process of searching out information for themselves in a natural way. This only requires oversight and management on the part of the parent, not a high-level degree. Like good managers, most parents oversee work they are not themselves qualified to do. They are, however, qualified to determine what is working and what is not, and to make executive decisions based upon that determination. So, my short answer to this question is yes, most parents are qualified to oversee their own children's educations.

"Shouldn't homeschooling parents be certified teachers?"

I am a certified teacher, so I feel I can speak, at least a little, to this subject. Many courses in teacher education are very useful to the home educating parent – especially developmental courses. On the other hand, I have learned a lot about teaching from my own children, and from other experienced homeschooling parents, that I did not learn in college. Since I do not have to face the challenges and constraints a schoolteacher faces, I don't have to approach teaching and learning in the same way. Thus, much of what I learned to become certified is not as applicable in a homeschool setting as it was for a group situation. Teaching my children in an unconventional way has helped me to think unconventionally, and that has been beneficial both to me and to my children.

I found that when I was going through my teacher education program, I was not as invested in the children put in my care as I am today. I wanted a good grade; I wanted to use the latest technology and research; I wanted to prove I could teach kids well, and I really wanted them to succeed academically; but, I didn't have the connection to my students in those 'practice' situations that I have with my own children. I did not have children then, and I didn't have the life experiences that have taught me how to choose lessons well. I knew how to act in a school environment, but I didn't know how to relate lessons to the real world very well. That reflected my own lack of experience.

My most valuable asset as a home educating parent is the fact that I am invested in my children. The second most valuable asset I have is the real world experience I have to share, and the new things I experience with them every day. Finally, while some of the techniques I learned in college have been of value to me, I know many parents who have learned most of these things through their experiences with their own children and their contact with other parents who teach. And, they have shown me some techniques I was not taught and had not learned in my teaching days. In fact, many homeschool parents consider it a benefit that they were not taught to think in a certain way. Most parents who home educate go out of their way to learn what they need to know in order to teach their own children, and sometimes it's best not to know where to start. That keeps you from limiting the possibilities. Much of what is taught in teacher training programs, such as how to ability-group or manage group behavior, is not particularly relevant to home education. Since studies indicate that certification of at least one parent has no statistically significant effect on the achievement of the children[1], my position that parents do not need to be certified even to be truly excellent home educators is well supported.

"What about poorly educated parents?"

Good question. This is one point that regularly gets brought up, because the educational attainment of parents is a big indicator of child achievement in the public schools.[2] This is also a factor in home education, but according to a study by Lawrence Rudner[3], children of poorly educated parents did better at home than they did in public schools.

Average students in public schools score around the 50th percentile on standardized tests by definition. Children of parents with low levels of formal education (high school education or less) typically score lower than average on these tests in public schools. Home educated students in this study whose parents had no college degree outperformed average students in public schools, achieving scores in the 65th to 69th percentile range. Since students educated at home scored in the 75th and 85th percentile range as a group, homeschooled children whose parents had less formal education lagged behind their peers who were taught at home, but were still ahead of their publicly-schooled peers. Thus, dedicated parents who were not very well educated themselves raised the educational standards for their children. It may reassure you to know, however, that home educating parents tend to have more formal education than the average parent in the United States.[4] According to Lawrence Rudner, "88% continued their educations beyond high school compared to 50% for the nation as a whole."

Parents also raise their own educational levels by teaching their own children. I've certainly learned a lot while teaching my children. Parents who are willing to learn can improve not only their children's educational prospects, but their own as well. It's not unusual for parents who didn't complete much of their formal education to go back to school at the same time they are teaching their children. What a positive example to set — that education is never done, and it is never too late to improve your own education level. This goes hand-in-hand with the common homeschool attitude that education is not something that is limited to certain hours of the day or years of your life, but is continuous, and never ceases.

Although home education may be harder for parents whose level of formal education is not very high, it certainly is not impossible for those who are motivated. In the process of searching out information to teach, learning how to teach it, and learning right along with their children, they pick up habits and experiences they did not get in school. Those who are not well-educated who do decide to homeschool seem to pour themselves into providing better experiences for their children than they had, and so make up for lack of prior knowledge in effort. This may account for their success in raising educated children.

"Don't most people homeschool because of religion?"

At one point, that was the stereotype of the typical home educator. And, many home educating parents do include religion as a reason they teach their children themselves. However, it is almost never the only reason, and it is increasingly not the main reason. Researchers in the 1980's and 1990's often contacted the people they studied from religious sources, or were themselves sponsored by religious organizations, thus producing a bias in the results. So, the only information the press had available to them was biased information, which was widely disseminated. In a 2003 United States Department of Education study, however, when asked to state their *main* reason for homeschooling, only 30 percent responded, "to provide religious or moral instruction." That means that 70 percent did NOT consider it their main reason. In the previous survey in 1999, respondents could give more than one reason for homeschooling. In that study, only 38.4 percent chose "religious reasons" as *one* of their reasons for homeschooling. In that case, over 60 percent did NOT choose religious reasons as *a* top rationale for home education. So, while religion does play a significant part in the education of many homeschool families, it is certainly not the only reason, or even the top reason for home educating, according to these surveys.

"What about being 'Salt and Light' to the public schools?"

Christian parents sometimes argue that if all the Christian kids leave the schools, the other kids will never hear about Jesus or see what Christ can do in a person's life. In my opinion, it is time to do a cost-benefit analysis of sending children in to do the work of adults. Most children do not have an adult understanding of Christianity, nor are they able to express themselves in a way that will convey what they do understand. Thus, the benefit to others, especially when sending small children to school, is negligible. More importantly, most children are vulnerable to peer pressure, and, if they've been raised to be respectful, will submit to adult authority in school. Thus, they are more likely to *be influenced* by the overriding tone of the school than to *influence* it. Since teachers are not officially allowed to endorse Christianity, even Christian teachers have to be careful how they express approval for a child's religious assertions, so any attempts children make to describe their religious views cannot be significantly reinforced at school.

Religion will only be notably reinforced at home or church, or in occasional contacts in the community.

However, many parents don't have much time just to talk with their children when they go to school. In my opinion, there are not more than a few Christian children out of a hundred who influence their peers more than their peers influence them, and that is a direct result of the involvement of the parents, both in the lives of their children and in the schools they attend.

Looking at this from a more Biblical view, Jesus included no children among His disciples. There is no mention of any of the seventy He sent out being children. He said, "Let the children alone, and do not hinder them from coming to Me; for the kingdom of heaven belongs to such as these."[4] He was speaking to their parents and to His disciples. He was saying it's OKAY for them to come to Him, but never did He say they should go to others and pass on their child-like faith. He called them to Himself, not to others. I believe He was instructing the adults to learn from their faith – not the children to teach it.

Matthew 21:15-16 says, "But when the chief priests and the scribes saw the wonderful things that He had done, and the children who were crying out in the temple and saying, "Hosanna to the Son of David," they became indignant, and said to Him, "Do You hear what these [children] are saying?" And Jesus said to them, "Yes; have you never read, 'OUT OF THE MOUTH OF INFANTS AND NURSING BABES THOU HAST PREPARED PRAISE FOR THYSELF'?"""

Even religious leaders tried to silence the children because they did not approve of what they said. The exuberant words a child may utter are often discredited at school. That puts a child in the awkward position of either disobeying authority or not sharing his or her religious thoughts and feelings. The official school position regarding religious expression, though unconstitutional, requires children to separate their religious observances from all others, which weakens them considerably and misses the point. Children also must endure much specifically anti-Christian teaching over time.

Most children cannot stand up to that pressure, especially over the course of seven or more hours a day for twelve years. Most adults could not stand up to it under the same circumstances. Jesus specifically called adults to be 'salt' and 'light' to the world in Matthew 5: 13-16. This means to reveal the truth of God's love in a clear and flavorful way at all times. It was a stern admonition that most adult Christians do not live out in their daily lives at work or elsewhere. Why should we send children to do what Jesus called us to do but we are afraid to do? WE, the ADULTS, need to be the salt and light in the schools. WE need to show our servant hearts. WE need to help where we are most needed. Even if we are not there to give a Christian witness, we can share love and our skills with children who desperately need it. Then our children will learn how to do that and be prepared in the next generation.

Perhaps Christian adults in America would love for children to do the hard work for them, but that is not what Jesus called them to do. I DO believe Christians should be integrally involved in our school systems, but not as children. Adults should make the effort to be the 'salt and light' they are expecting children to be.

"I couldn't homeschool - I'm not a fundamentalist Christian!"

So? Although there are specific Biblical reasons for parents to choose to teach their children at home, parents of many other religious backgrounds choose to home educate as well. There are support groups for most of them, too, if you're interested. Muslims, Jews, Pagans, Hindus, Buddhists, and others have formed homeschool support groups to help their members pass on their religious views to the next generation, as well as groups that are inclusive of multiple religious backgrounds. So, although many of the homeschool studies in the past have focused on Christian home educators, Christians are definitely NOT the only ones who homeschool, and Christians with fundamental views are not the only Christians who teach their children at home, either. Methodists, Catholics, Presbyterians, and other denominations have found or made comfortable niches for themselves in the home education community. There are also many home educators who do not adhere to any organized religious group.

Also, as I stated before, religion is not the number one reason cited in research as the reason parents choose to homeschool; the first reason named by parents is the environment at school. So, whether you have strong religious bonds or not, there are plenty of non-religious reasons to teach your children at home as well. And, there will be support for you from both religious and non-religious home educators to help you get started and keep going. Most of the materials used by school systems avoid Christian views, which makes finding non-Christian materials easy. In my opinion, some of the Christian materials written specifically for home education are the best designed. Since Christians used secular materials for years successfully, Christian materials are at least an option, and many will not overwhelm you with Christian doctrine.

"Can't you just teach your kids religion when they get home from school?"

Well, I suppose I could, and many parents do just that. It is very difficult to teach a way of thinking, however, and to demonstrate the power and presence of God after school. There are a few reasons why a parent might consider after-school teaching of religion inadequate. First, if you are a Christian, Jew, or Muslim, there are specific mandates to teach your own children the ways of God throughout the day, and not just at night and on Friday, Saturday, or Sunday. Deuteronomy 6: 6-7 is just one reference: "And these words, which I am commanding you today, shall be on your heart; and you shall teach them diligently to your sons and shall talk of them when you sit in your house and when you walk by the way and when you lie down and when you rise up." To not do so would violate a parent's agreement with God. And besides — it's pretty hard to do a good job in the few hours remaining after school.

Also, many would argue that religion is already taught diligently in the public schools, that it is in direct conflict with many other religions, and that it is hard to compete with. Religion? In OUR public schools? That's against the Constitution! Uh…Right? According to Webster's New Collegiate Dictionary, religion can mean "any specific system of belief and worship, often involving a code of ethics and a philosophy." That is clearly evident in our public schools.

The basic belief in our schools is that humans arose naturally, not as the result of any outside involvement, and are no better than any other life form. That gives rise to the philosophy that people must make their own decisions about what is right and good. The code of ethics is related to what is determined to be 'right,' and is generally considered to be what is seen as beneficial to people. This is called humanism.

If I were to ask you if schools endorsed sex education to prevent teen pregnancy, you would probably agree that they did. If we were to delve into it a little further, we might see that many schools do not see teen sex as the big problem, but only teen pregnancy. That reflects the schools' code of ethics. It details which types of solutions are acceptable, and which ones should be discarded. Abstinence is not considered a good solution because it is not seen as achievable for 'natural' beings.

Here's how that works out in real situations: if I teach, in my paltry few hours a week with my children, that sex outside of marriage is wrong and that life is sacred, but the school is demonstrating condom use and showing my children where to get abortions, there is a conflict of 'the code of ethics' that guide our religious practices. Since children are spending far more time steeped in the "system of belief" and "code of ethics and philosophy" of the public school system than they spend with parents, the task of sharing basis of your beliefs often becomes directed by counteracting the school's teachings. This becomes overwhelming and ineffective, and is more difficult than many parents want to tackle.

Well, at least our schools don't worship anything, do they? Here's a definition of worship, according to Webster's: "extreme devotion or intense love or admiration of any kind." For parents who have tried to change the way children in schools are educated, the "extreme devotion" of school systems both to humanism and to the educational philosophies that have shaped the way children are taught is obvious. No matter how much money is spent on schools or how many educational reforms take place, the philosophies that govern education remain essentially the same. Children still have days that are broken into subjects, and subjects that are broken into bite-sized lessons. They continue to be taken out of society to learn, without the benefit of seeing life in action. Testing is still a mainstay, and is even increasing in schools as the only true method of accountability and evaluation. Children continue to be moved systematically through the grades in groups, despite their differing needs and goals.

So, schools and their governing bodies do exhibit the characteristics of religious organizations. They have specific systems of belief to which they show extreme devotion, and display a code of ethics and philosophy in every curricular and programmatic choice made. This is difficult for parents with differing religious beliefs to counteract. Besides – why should they? If the academics are not superior, the social setting is not necessarily positive, the behavioral standards are not reinforcing adult behaviors, and school does not reinforce their most basic philosophies, why should parents send their children to school? Many parents don't think it is worth the effort.

Endnotes for chapter 10:

1. Rudner, 1999; and Ray, 1997.
2. Lara-Cinisomo et al, 2004.
3. Rudner, 1999.
4. Rudner, 1999; and USDE, 2001.
5. Matthew 19:14

All Grown Up — College And Other Topics

"Can homeschoolers really get into college?"

Yes, yes, and YES! They do it all the time! To see a list of colleges and universities that have accepted homeschoolers, please visit http://learninfreedom.org/colleges_4_hmsc.html. This is the *Colleges That Admit Homeschoolers FAQ* page on Karl M. Bunday's *Learn In Freedom* homeschooling website. This list represents confirmed admissions, is quite long, and gives you an idea of how many colleges are clearly open to students who have been educated at home. While some colleges are more inviting to homeschooled students than others, I cannot think of any colleges that would not at least consider the application of a home educated student in 2005.

Many colleges and universities actively recruit home educated students, and those that haven't in the past are changing their tunes – rapidly. Institutions of higher education are discovering that students taught at home bring a perspective to their campuses that is fresh and innovative, as well as experiences that students from institutional schools haven't had. Of course, it doesn't hurt that they also have higher average scores on standardized college tests like the SAT and the ACT.

Since transcripts can be a problem, however, many admissions counselors require portfolios or other 'proof' that the work they have done is college-preparatory. Wise parents overseeing the education of a high school student will check on the admission requirements at local colleges and universities when setting up a high school program. The more documentation a student has for work completed, the more reassured admissions counselors are about the course of study they have followed.

If you are considering home educating teens, there are many web pages dedicated to helping you prepare them for college. One of them is http://home schooling.gomilpitas.com/olderkids/OlderKids.htm. It is run by Ann Zeise, who is conscientious about updating her materials. You could probably find several links from her A to Z Home's Cool website that would match your situation, even if her approach does not match your philosophy.

"Can they get financial Aid for College?"

The easy answer to this is yes, but there are some glitches. A few years ago there was some information disseminated to colleges that contained inaccurate information about federal funding for colleges that admitted home educated students. According to the Home School Legal Defense Association, "Many homeschoolers have faced difficulty at various universities or college institutions during the 2001-2002 school year because some colleges refuse to admit homeschoolers for fear of losing their federal funding. The source of the problem? The Federal Student Aid Handbook that was issued during the last year of the Clinton administration contained inaccurate information. The Handbook indicated that colleges would lose their institutional eligibility if they admitted homeschool students. The Handbook was inaccurate and contradicted the federal law."[1]

A letter from the United States Department of Education cleared that up, but not until November of 2002. In the meantime many students were unfairly discriminated against. Occasionally something happens that puts another stumbling block in the way of home educating families, but for the most part the process is the same for homeschooled students as it is for students from any other educational background. It is important to work closely with the financial aid office of the institution and to leave plenty of time to spare, as with any student. Since more and more home educated students are continuing their educations at home through high school and are applying to college, most financial aid offices now have experience with home educated applicants.

"Can they get scholarships?"

Yes. Home educated students are well-represented among the ranks of National Merit Scholars, and are considered for most scholarships for which they are eligible (i.e., depending on their proposed areas of study, etc.). Parents of home educated high school students can clearly document their children's exceptionalities to increase their chances for scholarships.[2] Like any other scholarship search, of course, it is best to start early. It is not a bad idea to look at scholarships in the ninth or even eighth grade years, as well as the obvious junior year, to see if there are any scholarships that require a certain course of study or type of record-keeping that are of interest to your student. I am *not* proposing that you set up your program entirely to meet scholarship criteria. I *am* proposing that you consider that if some scholarship requirements closely match what you are already planning to do, you can do a little adjusting to your record-keeping or add a class to make sure of your student's eligibility.[3]

Sports scholarships are not out of range, either. I have a friend who has three sons who have earned baseball scholarships. It doesn't hurt that their dad is a scout for a major-league team, but that did not get them their scholarships. Like any other high school student seeking a sports scholarship opportunity, they sought out people who knew about the scholarship application process and followed their advice. They started early and made sure their sons were eligible for the school programs they wanted.

Many college recruiters are far more willing to look outside of school teams than they once were to find athletically-talented kids for their programs, and there are more places for them to look, too. Amateur Athletic Union (AAU) leagues come to mind. This is a program where extremely talented players are put together on regional teams that are not tied to school affiliation. Children from all educational backgrounds are included. The AAU basketball teams I know of are extremely competitive. So, there are options for athletically gifted students as well. All it takes is a little research and planning, which is what it takes for children in other school settings.

"Are they prepared for college, and how do they do academically when they get there?"

Many students are very ready, and many colleges are now actively recruiting home educated students as a result of their experiences. Of course, not all homeschoolers will be prepared, just as not all public or private school students will be. Whether or not they are prepared depends entirely upon whether or not they and their parents have been deliberately preparing for college. Just like any other secondary program, students can take a college preparatory or a general education track, depending upon the goals and aspirations of the student. Not all students are directing their educations at careers that require college degrees, and are preparing accordingly. Of those who do choose to attend college, many do very well and have truly impressed admissions counselors across the United States and Canada. This is quite an accomplishment, because colleges were somewhat dubious of the qualifications of home-schooled students in the past.

In the early 1990's there was a tendency on the part of professional educators to dismiss the possibility that the average home taught student could be prepared for college, although that perception was changing. Homeschool admissions to colleges were a new frontier in the world of higher education, and admissions counselors felt the brunt of the pressure that created. For some, it did not seem worth it to come up with guidelines for what seemed to be a relatively small number of very diverse applicants. Not many had bothered to investigate the research on home education available at the time.

Much has happened in the last decade or so, though. The number of home educated applicants has exploded. Homeschooling attracted positive media attention in 2000 when homeschooled students swept the top ranks of several national contests, and admissions counselors took notice. The positive standardized test results achieved by homeschoolers as a population became well known. More colleges and universities now have had experience with home educated students and have been pleased.

Homeschoolers are more appealing to colleges and universities now that so many are beginning to reach college age. The number of home educated high school students was relatively small during the earlier years of the movement. Parents are now more confident of their abilities to teach their own children at home, so more are teaching them right through high school graduation. It is clear that home educated students will not go away, and the dam is about to burst onto college campuses. I regularly read articles about the transition from home to college, and the overwhelming majority report high achievement, even when compared to the average college student. I expect that this trend will continue, even as the visibility of home educated students on campus increases.[7]

"How do they do socially and emotionally in college?"

Most homeschooled students who go to college have had some classroom experience before getting there, either in community classes, homeschool cooperatives, or tutorials, so that usually isn't much more stressful than for other freshmen. Research indicates that home educated students tend to be more secure as people than their group-schooled counterparts, so again, they are prepared to do well there, too.[4] In my experience, home educated teens tend to be more likely to seek out social interactions than other young people. They are used to forming clubs or joining them to find friends. They know how to be comfortable being alone when they need to. Since their social experience is more likely to mirror the kind of social situations found in college, I suspect they do pretty well. Unfortunately, there is not a lot of research in this area, but all the indicators are that they do very well. This is supported by information on college admissions web pages for home educated students, and by news articles describing the transition from living rooms to college campuses.

"How do they do in the military?"

This first part of section is based on a review of a military pilot program that started in 1999.[5] Home educated graduates were previously treated as Tier 2 recruits, which grouped them with less-desirable GED holders. This five-year pilot program granted them Tier 1 status, which is the same as for high school graduates, and followed their performance while enlisted. Here are some of the conclusions:

The recruits in this study had more dependents (that is, children of their own) than traditional high school graduates, and a higher than average incidence of waivers based on legal, alcohol, or drug problems. As a whole, this self-identified group of homeschoolers had considerably higher attrition rates when compared to public high school students. In this context, attrition refers to dropping out of the service and/or not fulfilling the contracted commitment. Some of the statistics about type of discharge and eligibility to reenlist were not inspiring, either. The results from this group were more characteristic of dropouts than typical homeschooled students. Not surprisingly, this particular subgroup of home educated graduates was not considered the most desirable set of recruits.

This represents the only study I have seen that uses documented information to compare homeschool graduates unfavorably with traditional school graduates, so I wanted to discuss it in greater detail. Surprisingly, there were some positives hidden in the pages of this review. Homeschooled recruits with better than average AFQT[6] scores had attrition rates similar to or slightly better than public school graduates. Graduates of home education programs who entered the Navy as "General Detail" recruits (GENDET), that is, not eligible to be rated for a specific specialty, were more likely than public school recruits to qualify for a rating at the end of 36 months. Having a rating means that recruits are eligible to remain in the Navy and serve in a specific job.

"Conversations with Navy representatives indicate that they believe the average quality of homeschooled recruits is much higher today than in [fiscal year 1999]... As of [fiscal year 2002], Navy homeschooled recruits average AFQT score was above 60." [7] There are several indications that the Navy recruits performed better than recruits who enlisted in the other branches. For example, the report begins with this disclaimer: "This document represents the best opinion of CNA at the time of issue. It does not necessarily represent the opinion of the Department of the Navy."[8]

In all, there were some unsettling statistics in that report. When

I first encountered this analysis, I was disturbed to find a study that used hard numbers to describe home educated students so negatively, in stark contrast to every other review I had ever encountered regarding students taught by their parents. However, as I read the study in greater depth, it became clear that the young people described in that group were not the same people described in other home education literature and research. For example, there were considerable problems classifying recruits accurately. Details in the report indicate that a large proportion of these students had spent two or fewer years homeschooling. Thus, the recruits' major educational influence was NOT from homeschooling. Those years must have been in high school to be considered homeschool graduates.

In my experience it is relatively rare for students to turn to home education for the first time in high school unless there are significant problems associated with staying in school such as pregnancy, chemical dependency, etc. Based upon the details associated with the recruits as a group, I have to assume that many of them turned to homeschooling as high school students to cope with a pre-existing crisis situation. Thus, it is my opinion that many of these recruits shared many characteristics with dropouts because they homeschooled to avoid dropping out of high school.

It does give me a reason to mention, however, that home education by itself does not guarantee good results, especially with short-term efforts. As with any endeavor, good results require dedicated, long-term, good old fashioned hard work. The journey of home education cannot become a fad or panacea embarked upon by the casual parent. It is not for the faint of heart or the lazy parent who equates home education with 'easy' results. It is best suited to those parents who have traditionally set out upon it — dedicated, deep, loving and concerned people with high principles who have a specific mission to train their children at home.

There are some other sources of information about how the military views home educated students, too. The United States Military Academy (West Point) declares itself "homeschooler friendly" on its website,[9] since it has accepted several home educated students upon their merits and found that many are great students. Military parents from all branches choose to home educate their own children. This seems to work well with the schedules and regular moves seen in military families. Various military academies are confirmed as having admitted home educated students according to Karl M. Bunday's "Colleges That Admit Homeschoolers" FAQ.[10] So, as always, it is important to look at both sides of the equation and do a little research. Although some self-reported homeschoolers prompted a negative report about their performance in the military, others have excelled.

Other information about home educated graduates:

The responses in the next section are mostly based on a 2003 research synopsis called *Homeschooling Grows Up*[11] by Dr. Brian D. Ray of the National Home education Research Institute (NHERI). This survey includes information from over 5000 adults who were home educated for at least seven years. The main reason I am using one study so heavily is that there simply aren't a lot of studies of home educated adults because of the length of time homeschooling has been widely recognized and legal in all 50 states. In fact, most of the adults surveyed in the NHERI sample were under the age of 30. Here are some questions based on the survey and a summary of the responses:

"How do they do when they graduate from high school?
Do they get good jobs?"

They do very well when they graduate. Because of the 'age' of the modern homeschool movement, nearly half (49 percent) of the homeschool graduates surveyed were still in college. In fact, over 74 percent of the homeschool graduates aged 18-24 had taken college-level classes, compared to the 46 percent of the general population that age in the United States. The rest had entered a wide variety of occupations. The only statistic that seemed different from the general population for these mostly young adults was that a large percentage (7.3 percent) reported that they were either home-makers or home educators. A 1991 study by J. Gary Knowles of 53 previously homeschooled adults showed that all had jobs and none required public assistance (welfare).

"Are they prepared to fit into society?"

Yes, they are. One of the greatest contrasts between adults who were home educated and the general population of adults in the United States is the level of community involvement demonstrated. 71 percent of the respondents participated in ongoing community service activities, compared to 37 percent of adults of similar ages. In fact, they were more involved in their communities and the political process in every possible way when compared to similarly aged adults. They voted more at every age level, but the contrast among young adults was the most striking: while 29 percent of young adults aged 18-24 as a whole voted in an election in the previous 5 years, 76 percent of previously home educated young adults had. They read more, watched TV less, visited the library more often, were members of more community groups and performed more community service than the population as a whole.

"Are they happy?"

Yup. 58.9 percent reported that they were "very happy," compared to 27.6 percent of the general population. Only 2 percent responded that they were "not too happy," compared to 9.4 percent of the population as a whole. They also felt that life was more exciting, they were more satisfied with their work, and they were more satisfied with their financial status than the general population. Over 95 percent reported that they were glad they had been homeschooled.

"Do they want to homeschool their own children?"

Yes, they do. This may be the most telling part of this survey. 82 percent reported that they would homeschool their own children, and of those who had children of school age, 74 percent were already doing so. That should not be surprising, because over 92 percent said that having been home educated was an advantage to them as adults. I also noticed when I was preparing the list of homeschoolers in history that parents who were deliberately home educated tended to at least try to educate their own children similarly.

Endnotes for chapter 11:

1. HSLDA, 2003 available from http://www.hslda.org/docs/news/hslda/200301/200301020.asp

2. Web sites that you might find helpful are: http://www.college-scholarships.com and http://www.hslda.org/docs/nche/Issues/C/College.asp.

3. A source of college admission policies and comments from college websites can be found on the A to Z Home's Cool webpage at http://home schooling.gomilpitas.com/olderkids/CollegeHSpages.htm.

4. Clicka, 2002.

5. Wenger and Hodari, 2004.

6. AFQT stands for Armed Forces Qualification Test. 50 is the average score.

7. From a footnote on page 39 of the study.

8. This statement was on the copyright page.

9. http://www.homeschoolfriendlycolleges.com/newyork/westpoint/wpoint.html

10. Karl M. Bunday's "Colleges That Admit Homeschoolers" FAQ can be found at: http://learninfreedom.org/colleges_4_hmsc.html.

11. *Homeschooling Grows Up* is a research synopsis by the Home School Legal Defense Association based upon a longer study by Dr. Ray entitled *Home Educated and Now Adults: Their Community and Civic Involvement, Views about Homeschooling, and Other Traits,* which is available through the National Home Education Research Institute at www.nheri.org.

In Conclusion

"I think this sounds great. How would I get started?"

If you are considering homeschooling, I would suggest doing three things: seeking guidance, deciding, and planning. *Seeking guidance* means researching homeschooling by reading a variety of materials about homeschooling, asking those who currently home-school specific questions, and praying. Find out what sounds good to you and what doesn't. Evaluate your own preferences as well as your child's. *Deciding* means making all this information personal. Are you willing to start? Do you *want* to homeschool, now that you know the facts? If so, make a decision to do it. Commit yourself to homeschool for at least a year. It is not beneficial to you or your child to be indecisive about this. *Planning* refers to selecting a method that will best fit you, your child, and your family. Consider finances, personalities, ages, and strengths and weaknesses. Not all homeschoolers are the same. Don't assume you will do things the same way your successful homeschooling neighbor does, because what works for that family may not be right for you. Make sure you include rest time in your plans, and find a source of personal support before you begin.

Each of these stages is essential in the process of creating an educational program to implement at home. Then, if you still decide you really want to homeschool, you must follow through. Do what you set out to do. The first year is the most difficult, especially if you are removing a child from a school situation, since you and your child are not only changing your lifestyles and ways of learning, you are also changing how you *think* about education. Being prepared for this can make it easier. As in any endeavor, though, perseverance is rewarded. Prepare to be flexible, positive, and committed, and you won't regret it.

"If I homeschool, I'll have great kids who do well academically, right?"

Nothing is guaranteed in life. Although the *average* student who is taught at home has fewer behavior problems and performs better on standardized tests than the *average* student who attends school, great kids don't just happen, no matter what program you subscribe to. Having the kind of kids you can be proud of takes consistent, involved, hard work over a long period of time; in other words, it takes good parenting.

Home education does not make you a good parent; it simply removes some of the barriers to good parenting that parents face today. It allows you more time with your children, so you can build good relationships with them and gently correct them before they get too far off track. It gives you the opportunity to provide consistent instruction over time, instead of hoping that 'this year' your child will have a good, kind teacher, or that the progress made in math this year will continue next year. You know it will, because you will make sure that it will. It gives you the chance to introduce the more confusing parts of the world on the timetable that works best for each of your individual children. It increases the time your child will spend with appropriate mentors, including you, and reduces the time your child will spend with inappropriate age-peers as mentors. It gives you a chance to really know your children well and see the importance of good parenting, and tends to increase your involvement in parenting in every way. In short, it gives you the opportunity to participate fully in raising your children. Very few parents enter into this responsible role casually, and those who do soon find themselves taking parenting more seriously, since homeschooling has challenges of its own. So, while home education certainly does not guarantee success, it does provide good parents with more opportunities for success.

Well, I hope I've given you something to think about. Homeschooling can be a great way to learn and to educate your children. It's definitely not for everyone, and that's appropriate, but it is very successful for many of us. I hope I've given you some insight into why we do this strange thing we do with our children, and I hope you've been reassured that we are normal people who have made a viable educational decision. This book was never intended to convince diehard critics to support home education; it *was* intended to help the critics and the puzzled alike to better understand it. It is my sincere hope that I have done that.

A Few Internet Resources for Home Educators

* Note: I cannot possibly provide an exhaustive list of resources in this small space. They would probably be outdated by the time the book was published, anyway! However, I tried to provide enough stable and reputable resources and links that you can look some things up for yourselves. My listing of resources here does not mean that I agree with everything listed on the websites, and websites are listed alphabetically — not necessarily in the order in which I recommend you visit them. I have also avoided listing sites or resources that I am not personally somewhat familiar with, so you may have to do Internet searches yourself to find information specifically suited to you. What I have is a start, though. Happy hunting!

- **A Beka (distance education and materials): http://www.abeka.org**
- **A to Z Home's Cool (detailed homeschool information and resources): http://homeschooling.gomilpitas.com**
- **African American Homeschoolers Network: http://www.aahnet.org**
- **Calvert School (distance education for elementary school): http://www.calvertschool.org**
- **Catholic Homeschool Support: www.catholichome-school.org**
- **Christian Book Distributors (new homeschool supplies):**

http://christianbook.com or
http://www.christianbook.com (click on the homeschool
link at the top of the page)

- **Christian Liberty Academy (K-12 distance education):**
  http://www.homeschools.org
- **Home School Legal Defense Association (general homeschool information and resources, as well as legal information):** www.hslda.org or www.hslda.com
- **Jostens (source for homeschool ceremonial items; just
  click on "homeschool" before browsing):**
  http://www.jostens.com
- **Learn In Freedom website (detailed homeschool information and resource links):** http://www.learninfree-
  dom.org
- **Mocha Moms (supporting stay-at-home mothers of
  color):** http://www.mochamoms.org
- **National African-American Homeschoolers Alliance:**
  www.naaha.com/
- **National Challenged Homeschoolers Associated
  Network –NATHHAN (homeschooling special needs
  children):** http://www.nathhan.com/
- **National Foundation for Gifted and Creative Children:**
  http://www.nfgcc.org
- **National Home Education Research Institute:**
  www.nheri.org/
- **Sonlight (curriculum and message boards):**
  www.Sonlight.com
- **Tennessee HomeEd (general homeschool information in
  Tennessee):** www.TnHomeEd.com
- **Timberdoodle (homeschool supplies):**
  http://www.timberdoodle.com
- **Vegsource discussion boards (message boards and used
  homeschool materials):**
  http://www.vegsource.com/homeschool

Bibliography

Alden, D. (1998). *Are we teaching American Citizens or training Prussian Serfs? from a speech by Senator Ann O'Connell.* Nevada Journal. Retrieved July 11, 2005, from http://nj.npri.org/nj98/05/prussian.htm

Basham, P., (2001). *Home Schooling: From the Extreme to the Mainstream.* Public Policy Sources, Number 51. Frasier Institute Occasional Paper. Retrieved June, 2005 from http://www.fraserinstitute.ca/admin/books/files/homeschool.pdf

Bielick, S., Chandler, K., and Broughman, S. P., (2001). *Homeschooling in the United States: 1999* (NCES 2001-033). U. S. Department of Education. Washington, DC: National Center for Education Statistics.

Bielick, S., and Princiotta, D., (2004). *1.1 Million Homeschooled students in the United States in 2003* (NCES 2004-115). Issue Brief. U. S. Department of Education. Washington, DC: National Center for Education Statistics.

Burnham, J. (2005, January). *Faculty Liberal Bias Often Subtle, Intrinsic.* The Daily Texan. Retrieved July 16, 2005, from http://www.dailytexanonline.com/media/paper410/news/2005/01/27/Opinion/Faculty.Liberal.Bias.Often.Subtle.Intrinsic-842783.shtml

Catalanello, R. (June 26, 2005). *Homeschooling: It's Not What You Think*. St. Petersburg Times Online. Retrieved July 10, 2005, from http://www.sptimes.com

Centers for Disease Control and Prevention. National Center for Injury Prevention and Control. *Child Maltreatment: Fact Sheet*. Retrieved June 30, 2005, from http://www.cdc.gov/ncipc/fact-sheets/cmfacts.htm

Clicka, C., (2002). *Socialization: Homeschoolers Are in the Real World* retrieved June 14, 2005, from http://www.hslda.org/docs/nche/000000/00000068.asp

Crnic, K., & Lamberty, G. (1994). *Reconsidering School Readiness: Conceptual and Applied Perspectives*. Early Education and Development, April 1994, Volume 5, Number 2, retrieved June 14, 2005, from http://readyweb.crc.uiuc.edu/library/1994/crnic1.html

Devoe, J. F., Peter, K., Kaufman, P. Ruddy, S. A., Miller, A. K., Planty, M., Snyder, T. D., and Rand, M. R. (2003). *Indicators of School Crime and Safety: 2003*. NCES 2004-004/NCJ 201257. U. S. Departments of Education and Justice. Washington, DC: 2003. Retrieved July 28, 2005, from http://www.ojp.usdoj.gov/bjs/pub/pdf/iscs03.pdf

Gallager, T., and Jonas, S. (2003, May 21) *Home schooling on the Rise in Black Communities*. Fox News. Retrieved May, 2003, from http://www.foxnews.com/story/0,2933,87494,00.html

Gatto, J. *The Underground History of American Education*. Retrieved July 7, 2005 from http://www.johntaylorgatto.com/underground

Gatto, J. *The Public School Nightmare*. Retrieved July 15, 2005, from the Diablo Valley School website at http://www.dvschool.org/psngatto.htm, linked from The Preservation Institute at http://www.preservenet.com/theory/Gatto.html

History 101. (April 28, 2001). World Magazine. Volume 16, Number 16. Retrieved July 12, 2005, from http://www.worldmag. com/displayarticle.cfm?id=4957

Home School Legal Defense Association. (2003, January). Breakthrough For Homeschoolers Seeking College Admission And Financial Aid. Retrieved July 29, 2005, from http://www.hslda.org/ docs/news/hslda/200301/200301020.asp

Home School Legal Defense Association. (2004, February). *NCAA Eliminates Waiver Process For Homeschoolers.* Retrieved June 15, 2005, from http://www.hslda.org/docs/news/hslda/200402/ 200402090.asp

Homeschool Legal Defense Association. (2004, October). *Academic Statistics on Homeschooling.* Retrieved June, 2005 from http://www.hslda.org/docs/nche/000010/200410250.asp

Johnson, F. (2005). *Revenues and Expenditures by Public School Districts: School Year 2001-2002* (NCES 2005-342). U.S. Department of Education. Washington, DC: National Center for Education Statistics.

Kettler, R., and Valentine, J., (2000). *NMSA Research Summary # 18: Parent Involvement and Student Achievement at the Middle Level (2000).* National Middle School Association. Retrieved June 16, 2005, from http://www.nmsa.org/research/ressum18.htm

Kite, M. (2004, February 15). *Children should learn more about atheism and less about Jesus, says Labour think-tank.* News.Telegraph. Retrieved February, 2004 from http://news.tele-graph.co.uk/news/main.jhtml?xml=/news/2004/02/15/nedu15.xml

Kohn, A. (1999, March). *From Degrading to De-Grading.* High School Magazine. Retrieved June 15, 2005, from http://www.alfiekohn.org/teaching/fdtd-g.htm

Kraychir, H. R. (2003, July). *Dispelling the Stereotype of Ethnic*

Prejudice in Homeschooling. Retrieved June 15, 2005, from http://homeschooling.gomilpitas.com/articles/071003.htm

Kurtz, H. (2005, March). *College Faculties A Most Liberal Lot, Study Finds.* Washington Post.com. Retrieved July 16, 2005, from http://www.washingtonpost.com/wp-dyn/articles/A8427-2005Mar28.html

Lara-Cinisomo, S., & Pebley, A. R., & Vaiana, M. E., & Maggio, E., & Berends, M., & Lucas, S. R. (2004, Fall). *A Matter of Class: Educational Achievement Reflects Family Background More Than Ethnicity or Immigration,* retrieved June 13, 2005 from http://www.rand.org/publications/randreview/issues/fall2004/class.html

Lines, P. (1999, Spring). *Homeschoolers: Estimating Numbers and Growth,* National Institute on Student Achievement, Curriculum, and Assessment. Office of Educational Research and Improvement. U.S. Department of Education, retrieved June 11, 2005 from http://www.ed.gov/offices/OERI/SAI/homeschool/homeschoolers.pdf

McCoy, J. *Calculating the True Cost of Working Versus Full-Time Parenting.* Parenthood.com. Retrieved July 19, 2005, from http://www.parenthood.com/articles.html?article_id=1000

National Education Association. *Getting Involved in Your Child's Education,* retrieved June 13, 2005, from http://www.nea.org/parents/index.html

National Education Association (2004). *Some NEA Resolutions passed at 2004 Convention in Washington, DC.* Education Reporter. Retrieved June 14, 2005 from the Eagle Forum website at http://www.eagleforum.org/educate/2004/aug04/NEA-resolutions.html

Ray, B. D. (1997). *Home Education Across the United States,* retrieved June 14, 2005, from http://www.hslda.org/docs/study/ray1997/default.asp

Ray, B. D. (2003). *Homeschooling Grows Up*. Home School Legal Defense Association's Synopsis of *Home Educated and Now Adults: Their Community and Civic Involvement, Views about Homeschooling, and Other Traits*. National Home Education Research Institute. Salem, Oregon.

Richman, S. (1994). *Separating School & State: How To Liberate American Families*, Chapter 3: Why There Are Public Schools. Future of Freedom Foundation. Retrieved June 13, 2005, from http://www.sntp.net/education/school_state_3.htm

Rudner, L. M., (1999). *Scholastic Achievement and Demographic Characteristics of Home School Students in 1998*. ERIC Clearinghouse on Assessment and Evaluation. College of Library and Information Services. University of Maryland, College Park. Report obtained from Home School Legal Defense Association website. Retrieved June, 2005 from http://www.hslda.org/docs/study/rudner1999/FullText.asp

Smith, J. M., (2004, April 14). *Homeschooling Strengthens Families and Communities*. Washington Times Editorial, collected on the Internet April 14, 2004

Starr, L. (2000, July 11). *Sticks and Stones and Names Can Hurt You: De-Myth-tifying the Classroom Bully!* Education World. Retrieved July 27, 2005 from http://www.education-world.com/a_issues/issues102.shtml

U. S. Department of Education. National Center for Education Statistics. (1997). *1996 National Household Education Survey (NHES:96) Questionnaires: Screener/Household and Library, Parent and Family Involvement in Education and Civic Involvement, Youth Civic Involvement, and Adult Civic Involvement*, Working Paper No. 9725. Project Officer, Kathryn Chandler. Washington, D.C.: 1997.

U. S. Department of Education. National Center for Education Statistics. (2000) *Issues relating to Estimating the Home-Schooled*

Population in the United States With National Household Survey Data, NCES 2000-311, by Robin R. Henke and Phillip Kaufman. Project officers: Steven P. Broughman and Kathryn Chandler. Washington, DC: 2000.

U. S. Department of Education. National Center for Education Statistics. *The Condition of Education 2000-2005*. Retrieved June 13, 2005, from http://nces.ed.gov/programs/coe

Wenger, J. W., and Hodari, A. K., (2004). *Final Analysis of Evaluation of Homeschool and ChalleNGe Program Recruits*, CRM D0009351.A2/final, CNA, Alexandria, Virginia, 2004. Retrieved June 16, 2005, from http://www.cna.org/documents/D0009351.A2.pdf

Printed in the United States
59992LVS00003B/163-165

9 781597 815727